PRAISE *for* MATTHEW HENNESSEY

What we badly need right now is someone to remind us of what economic freedom is and does. Matthew Hennessey's *Visible Hand* is a wise reminder that free markets are essential to human flourishing. In an engaging and highly amusing style he boils economic concepts down to their essence. Buy this for any son or daughter who needs to know what American capitalism is, what it isn't, and why its departure would bring great ill.

—**Peggy Noonan,** Wall Street Journal *columnist*

Matthew Hennessey makes the case for liberal democracy and American capitalism in plain English—and he does it with a sense of humor, too. Nothing dismal here. Econ 101 should always be this much fun.

—**Larry Kudlow,** *former director of the National Economic Council*

Matthew Hennessey brings to economics the sensibility of a man who grew up helping to tend bar at his father's saloon in New Jersey: He has no interest in putting on airs, only in telling you the story. In *Visible Hand* he has produced the most completely enjoyable book on economics I've ever encountered. Economics? Enjoyable? Did I just write that? Because of Matt, I did.

—**Peter Robinson,** *Murdoch Distinguished Policy Fellow at the Hoover Institution*

As a libertarian, I don't like mandates, but *Visible Hand* should be required reading for every American. It will restore faith in the power of capitalism to increase opportunity for all of us, especially those born without wealth and privilege. For too long, economics has been the province of writers of gray prose and makers of two-dimensional supply-and-demand charts. Hennessey uses personal experience, history, and popular culture to create a thrilling story about how the world actually works. I'm going to make my sons—a Millennial and a Zoomer—read *Visible Hand*, which explains how individualism, free markets, choice, and entrepreneurial risk make us richer, happier, and more fulfilled.

—**Nick Gillespie,** *Editor at Large,* Reason

This delightful and entertaining book makes the ideas behind economics accessible to all. It also reminds both novices and econ wonks why economic reasoning is so important and critical to understanding the world today.

—**Allison Schrager,** *Manhattan Institute Senior Fellow*

VISIBLE
HAND

A WEALTH OF NOTIONS *on the*
MIRACLE OF THE MARKET

HAND

MATTHEW HENNESSEY

Encounter
BOOKS
New York · London

© 2022 by Matthew Hennessey

All rights reserved. No part of this publication may be reproduced, stored in a retrieval system, or transmitted, in any form or by any means, electronic, mechanical, photocopying, recording, or otherwise, without the prior written permission of Encounter Books, 900 Broadway, Suite 601, New York, New York, 10003.

First American edition published in 2022 by Encounter Books, an activity of Encounter for Culture and Education, Inc., a nonprofit, tax-exempt corporation.
Encounter Books website address: www.encounterbooks.com

Manufactured in the United States and printed on acid-free paper. The paper used in this publication meets the minimum requirements of ANSI/NISO Z39.48Ð1992 (R 1997) (*Permanence of Paper*).

FIRST AMERICAN EDITION

LIBRARY OF CONGRESS CATALOGING-IN-PUBLICATION DATA

Names: Hennessey, Matthew, 1973- author.
Title: Visible Hand: A Wealth of Notions on the Miracle of the Market / by Matthew Hennessey.
Description: First American edition. | New York, NY: Encounter Books, 2022. | Includes bibliographical references and index. |
Identifiers: LCCN 2021034947 (print) | LCCN 2021034948 (ebook) | ISBN 9781641772372 (hardcover) | ISBN 9781641772389 (ebook)
Subjects: LCSH: Economics--Popular works.
Classification: LCC HB171 .H54 2022 (print) | LCC HB171 (ebook) | DDC 330--dc23
LC record available at https://lccn.loc.gov/2021034947
LC ebook record available at https://lccn.loc.gov/2021034948

*For my father,
who gave me everything*

CONTENTS

Introduction vii

CHAPTER 1: The Miracle 1

CHAPTER 2: Markets 25

CHAPTER 3: Motivations 43

CHAPTER 4: Preferences 63

CHAPTER 5: Prices 79

CHAPTER 6: Specialization 111

CHAPTER 7: Work 129

CHAPTER 8: Business 145

CHAPTER 9: The Anti-Marketeers 177

CHAPTER 10: Gravitation 209

Afterword 217
Acknowledgments 221
Index 225

INTRODUCTION

I am not an economist. I'm telling you that now, here at the beginning, because you have a right to know what kind of person you're dealing with.

This is a book about economics, broadly speaking, and some would say I'm out of my depth. Fair enough. I'm not licensed. I don't have a PhD in economics. I don't have a PhD in anything. The gatekeepers of the vast edifice of economic knowledge tend not to look kindly on the opinions of the uncredentialed. They like to keep it complicated. They prefer to dress economic things up in opaque terminology and technical jargon, stashing it all on a high college shelf, well out of the reach of the average person. This book is not for them.

I don't pretend to be making a contribution to the academic literature. This isn't a dissertation or a textbook. It's just one guy's view of the world through market-colored glasses. Don't say I didn't warn you.

There's more you should know: I've never worked in business, banking, finance, or—until relatively recently—a large private company. I couldn't tell you a single useful thing about accounting other than that assets equal liabilities plus equity on the balance sheet and that people who study accounting in college tend to nab high-paying jobs right out of the gate. I don't know how to read an earnings report and I'm useless with a spreadsheet. Stocks don't interest me much, apart from the possibility that they will pay for my retirement. Cryptocurrency might as well be professional lacrosse for all I care about it, which is not very much. I don't think the world revolves around career, money, bond prices, or the oil market.

After reading a list of all my non-qualifications, you may be wondering why I have written a book on economics at all. I did it because I suspect many people are afraid of economics, or confused and intimidated by it, just like I once was. For most of my life I avoided the topic entirely. Then I woke up one day and realized that all I'd been doing my whole life was acting like an economist: responding to incentives, weighing trade-offs, making decisions at the margin, and calculating the utility of everything from investing in my education to helping myself to a second scoop of strawberry ice cream. So this is a book about economics for people who, broadly speaking, don't like economics. Or think they don't.

Introduction

I'm the sort of fellow who thinks American-style capitalism works pretty damn well most of the time, especially when alternatives are considered. It has its quirks, it has its shortcomings, it even has its failures, but free markets have over the past three centuries lifted billions of people out of poverty in every corner of the globe. That's not a meaningless statement. Real people, as alive as you or me, who would otherwise have lived solitary, poor, nasty, brutish, and short lives, instead lived good lives, fruitful lives, healthy lives, prosperous lives—all thanks to the material improvements made possible by free markets.

It happened in my own family. My parents grew up poor. My dad was born during the Depression. He wore clothes with holes in them. My mother was born in the mid-1940s. She lived in a house with no indoor plumbing. In later life my parents managed to push their way solidly into the middle class. As owners of a small local business, they made enough money to allow them to take relaxing vacations. They visited Turks and Caicos. They once went to Hawaii. They visited England, Scotland, and Wales. They traipsed around France. They crisscrossed Ireland, their common ancestral homeland, in search of the source of the jigs and reels that gave rhythm to their hearts. These were the kinds of holidays that their own parents could never have dreamed possible. Eventually they sold their old, cold house on a busy road and decamped for the tranquility of the New Jersey countryside, such as it is. My mother spent her final years puttering around in a biggish flower garden. My dad loved nothing more than to sit on his spacious and well-shaded deck with a book on his lap as he dozed to the sounds of the forest.

Only in America.

And only in hindsight can I see how their life's work was accomplished, how they built a good thing in this world—an enterprise, if you like—and sustained it even as it sustained them and a great many people who came into contact with it and with them. My parents owned a business, but they didn't consider themselves *businesspeople*. Then again, everyone is in business, as legendary *Wall Street Journal* editor Barney Kilgore liked to say— the business of making a living.

My main goal here is to clarify a few things, to make economics, broadly speaking, seem a little less frightening for anyone who does their best to avoid it as a matter of mental and emotional hygiene. I address what might fairly be called the basics—choice, competition, incentives, scarcity, trade-offs, supply and demand, prices, utility, etc. At various times I present my parents' small business as a sort of case study for how a profit-seeking enterprise can provide social goods. And not just a single or limited social good like generating an income for a family but a cascade of social goods, like spreading happiness, holding a community together, and increasing the general welfare.

In recent years free markets have come under fire from both left and right. Both criticisms need dealing with, and I will give it a go, but the greater problem across every level of American society is a simpler one: ignorance. Most people don't even know what a market is, much less what makes one free. They shut down when they hear the words "capitalism" or "economics." They tune out. They start thinking about what's for dinner or humming something they heard on the radio. I know they do, because I used to be one of them.

CHAPTER 1

THE MIRACLE

There are things in life that you manage to miss. Many dedicated music lovers don't know what a bass guitar is or why every rock band must necessarily include one. A friend of mine has never seen *The Godfather*, so you can't tell him to take the cannoli and leave the gun and expect him to get the reference.

We all have blind spots. Fitness trends, literary allusions, crystal structure, automotive science, nose-to-tail eating—there's no end to the things that some people have deep knowledge and strong opinions about but that might, for one reason or another, fail to register on your radar. It could be that nobody ever told you about the bass guitar. Could be that some people are too busy with their doctoral studies or training for marathons or raising three kids to sit down and watch *The Godfather*. Could be that you just don't care about lattice parameters and waste-not, want-not culinary trends like eating a whole animal. There's only so much room for particle physics in most brains.

Then, whether by accident, by education, or because somebody happens to flick on the lights, all of a sudden you notice that thing that you somehow always managed to miss. In the snap of a finger, you get it, you can see why it matters, and you wonder how you could have been so blind for so long.

"Was this here the whole time?" you ask, thrilled by your discovery. "Did everybody know but me?"

From that moment on, as if your life has been scripted by a screwball screenwriter, you start seeing that once-invisible thing everywhere. In your work and in your leisure. In what you read and in the conversations you have with friends. On television and on the internet. That thing you somehow managed to miss all your life starts popping up wherever you look. Sometimes when you see it you feel a low and glowing pride sprouting from your newfound knowledge—you're in the club now, after all, among those who (*wink wink*) can see what all those dummies somehow still manage to miss.

The Blindness Is the Hardest Part

For most of the early part of my life, economics was something that I did my best to avoid. Whatever it was—and, for a long time, I didn't really know what it was—economics struck me as the kind of thing that my brain didn't have room for. It sounded like homework to me. It had the whiff of math. I wanted nothing to do with it. I wanted to keep all jibber-jabber about market movements, interest rates, oil futures, home prices, mortgages, tariffs, and trade as far away from my ears as possible.

When you really want not to learn about something, it's remarkably easy to succeed. My parents didn't talk much about such things. Nobody at school did either, except in the vaguest of terms. When the newspaper came I skipped right to the sports section. When the nightly news did a story on agricultural subsidies or the challenge to the auto industry from Japan, I'd get up and go to the kitchen for a glass of water. At least once a day I caught a quick mental nap when someone on the radio mentioned the Dow Jones Industrial Average. *Zzzzzzz.*

In October 1987 the stock market crashed. I was a freshman in high school, and I had no idea what had happened or why it mattered. In 1992 James Carville became a household name for saying, "It's the economy, stupid." I was 19 and I had no idea what that meant. Didn't know, didn't care. To me, the economy was like the weather. Complex. Of mysterious origin. The people who talked about it were the most boring set of nerd jockeys you could imagine. Like the weather, you couldn't do anything about the economy. You couldn't predict it. You couldn't explain it. All you could do was complain about it. Economics was for me a byword for disaster. It was the thing that adults blamed their problems on.

While I wasn't much interested in economics in the early years, economics was interested in me. Like death, taxes, and gravity, economics is interested in all of us.

It's All About the Trade-Offs

An example: I've always been a ham. As a kid I loved getting up in front of the class to speak or read, and I always, always went out for the school play. If you don't mind me saying so, I was pretty adept at the thespianical arts, so I usually got a sizable part in whatever play (or playlet) happened to be that season's showcase. When I got to high school, I couldn't wait to audition for the musical comedies and serious dramas. This was like the major leagues to me. I dreamed of becoming the proverbial big man on campus for at least one weekend in the fall, when the school put on a straight play, and two weekends in the spring, which was the season for the annual senior follies.

But I had a problem. I played sports—soccer and baseball—and I was good at those too, especially baseball. Kids play these sports year-round now, but when I was growing up soccer was a fall deal and baseball a spring affair. The after-school rehearsals for the shows I wanted to do conflicted with the game and practice schedules of the sports I wanted to play. If I did the show, I couldn't play soccer or baseball. If I played baseball or soccer, I couldn't do the show. There was no way around it. I chose to do the shows. It was a disappointment, because I loved sports and wanted to play, but I couldn't be in two places at once. Still can't.

I know what you're thinking: What's this got to do with economics? A fair question, and one I would have surely demanded an answer to back when the sound of that word was to me like the squeal of microphone feedback. What does my struggle to choose an extracurricular activity in high school have to do with what some people call "the dismal science"? Only everything. My dilemma wasn't really about baseball and the school play. It was a matter of balancing trade-offs. To choose one option meant giving up another option. You can't have everything you want. That's the heart of economics.

Something to bear in mind as you read on: There's no need to be intimidated by numbers, percentages, and statistics, because there won't be any. There's no reason to shut down, as I once did, when people start talking about markets. There's no reason to be embarrassed that you don't know what an index fund is or how the global price of oil is set. Hang not your head. Economics may not be what you thought it was at all. The key economic questions aren't numerical or statistical. Frequently they don't even have anything to do with money. They have to do with choice.

Adam Smith's Hand

You have heard, perhaps, of the "invisible hand" of the marketplace. Your high school European history teacher may have mentioned it on the day devoted to discussion of the Industrial Revolution. If so, you probably got your diploma knowing about as much about supply and demand as you did about the Teapot Dome scandal or the Zimmermann telegram. That is to say, bubkes.

The invisible hand is a popular clue in crossword puzzles. Maybe you've come across it there. Someone in college may have told you that a Scotsman named Adam Smith came up with the idea of the invisible hand as a way of explaining his theory that society somehow benefits from the selfish actions of greedy people. Perhaps you read a sneering column about invisible hands in the *New York Times*, mocking trickle-down economists and supply-side charlatans for their cult-like belief in the healing power of business and commerce.

Someone may have told you that the invisible hand is nothing but a myth, a trick played by robber barons and Republicans to help them line their pockets. If you're at all like me, when you hear someone mention the invisible hand you can't help but imagine a giant foam finger pushing shoppers from one store to another at the mall. I hope you're not like me.

If no one told you the truth about the invisible hand, I'll do it now. Adam Smith did come up with the idea. That much is true. He mentioned the invisible hand, once, in an offhanded sort of a way, in his bread-loaf-sized masterpiece *The Wealth of Nations*, which hit bookshelves in 1776, the same year as Thomas Jefferson's Declaration of Independence. While modern readers understandably turn green after one look at Smith's archaic prose style—"An intercourse of the same kind universally established between the farmers and the corn merchants, would be attended with effects equally beneficial to the farmers"—it's hard to think of a work written in the last 500 years that's done more to help the world understand itself.

The Wealth of Nations is, to put it mildly, an important book, and at the risk of sounding like a smarty-pants, let me suggest that an educated person should read it. Someone who merely wishes to appear educated when friends drop by should at the very least have it on his bookshelf, even if he only intends to read it one day when his phone dies or a block of 40 straight days of nothing opens up on his calendar.

Smith is sometimes called the father of modern capitalism, a nickname that carries with it the odor of invention. Attendant to this notion is that before Smith came along with his invisible hand, there existed none of the market forces that we normally associate with classical economics. Some go so far as to posit that a reasonably happy pre-Enlightenment harmony obtained among the peasantry and the aristocracy of western Europe. This imagined equilibrium rested on noblesse oblige and a strong social compact, subsistence farming, local market days, and a modicum of international trade for luxuries like coffee, tobacco, and wine. Just as the Declaration of

Independence signaled the birth of a new and exciting brand of democratic political organization that would disrupt the old order of things, so, in the minds of some, did *The Wealth of Nations* announce that laissez-faire capitalism had come to town, ready to join forces with colonialism to smash and grab all it could on the way to world domination.

If all you ever got from that high school European history teacher was that the Industrial Revolution moved people off the land (where they were poor but happy) and into the factories (where they were poor and miserable), you can be forgiven for thinking that the whole capitalist project was Adam Smith's doing. If that's where you're coming from you probably feel justified laying every sin of capitalism from the British East India Company to Enron—not to mention reality TV, climate change, and Flamin' Hot Cheetos Puffs—at the venerated Scotsman's feet.

Adam Smith didn't invent free markets any more than Thomas Jefferson invented representative democracy or Isaac Newton invented gravitation, so let's absolve him of responsibility for all the things you don't like about modern American life, whether it's consumer culture or noise pollution. Obviously Smith, Newton, and Jefferson each did the world a huge favor by devoting himself to the promotion and refinement of his particular area of interest.

But the work is better described as "revelation" rather than "invention." The Declaration of Independence assumes and pays homage to truths that are self-evident. Newtonian physics illuminates and describes the effects of physical forces at play on material bodies. These are revelatory contributions to the sum of human knowledge. Through the power of the written word and the language of mathematics, Jefferson and Newtown made visible what previously had been invisible.

So, too, did Adam Smith. In *The Wealth of Nations* he wrote the plain truth about how humans live, work, play, and interact with each other *as he observed it*. Smith took the world as it was and reflected it back to itself. He illuminated the darkness. *The Wealth of Nations* isn't theory; it's closer to journalism. Smith reports on the things that people do. He breaks down how we behave in economic situations—that is to say, how we assign value to goods, how we produce and trade them, how we work, how we spend time productively, how we organize our lives. Smith is an explorer, a discoverer, not an inventor or a revolutionary. He's interested in what motivates us to produce or not to produce, to work or not to work, to trade or not to trade. Most of the time this boils down to whether we'll do a little more or a little less. He's interested in our motivations and how our actions affect others.

That's what economics is, and it's a far cry from the picture that your high school history teacher probably painted of Adam Smith and the invisible hand associated with his name. Granted, there's a lot of economic illiteracy baked in to the American education system. Basic economics is not typically a required subject, either in high school or college, so falsehoods and distortions about what it is and why it matters have plenty of room to run in American culture. You could easily live to a ripe old age without ever hearing the term "marginal utility." Rare is the teenager who can tell you what prices are or how they are set. Rarer still is the adult who can explain why laws against price gouging lead to shortages of crucial goods in difficult times.

Personally, I didn't encounter Adam Smith and his ideas until I was nearly 30 years old, at which time I found them so compelling and self-evident that I felt instantly betrayed by the people who educated me.

"How could no one have told me about this?"

Then I remembered that just about everyone I've ever known was in the same boat. We all have the same blind spot. In this regard, the invisible hand is aptly named.

The funny thing is that Smith used the most well-known metaphor in economics as a throwaway. Buried deep, deep within the never-ending prose blob of *The Wealth of*

Nations, in a passage devoted to the "restraints upon the importation from foreign countries of such goods as can be produced at home"—aka import duties, or tariffs—the invisible hand raises itself ever so briefly. A person who "intends only his own gain is . . . in this, as in many other cases, led by an invisible hand to promote an end which was no part of his intention." That's it. Smith never mentions nor refers to it again, and believe me when I tell you that few books contain as many words as *The Wealth of Nations* does. It really is remarkable that the invisible hand has evolved into a shorthand for free market economics. Whoever first decided that it represented the essence of Smith's thinking was reading very, very closely.

As a teaching tool, the invisible hand has its uses. Buyers and sellers in a free market do tend to find what they're looking for as if pushed along by invisible magic forces, and those magic forces do have secondary effects that yield benefits to society as a whole. But more often the metaphor has been misunderstood, misinterpreted, and twisted such that in most people's eyes it has come to mean, basically, that greed is good, that anything goes where profit is concerned, that the business of America is business, and all that jazz. None of that is true or fair. Smith wasn't attempting anything more ambitious with the metaphor than this: "By pursuing his own interest [every person] frequently promotes that of the society more effectually than when he really intends to promote it." Doing what's good for you often is the best thing you can do for society. That doesn't mean that people can't or shouldn't try to promote society's interests, however they are defined. Lots do and some succeed. I think Adam Smith would be all for it. He is simply saying that, most of the time, pursuing your own interest does the overall job better and comes with the added benefit of satisfying your needs. Everything we know about the world proves that this observation is true. The astonishing thing is that no one thought of it before Smith.

My Miseducation and Yours

I went to high school in the late 1980s. It was the Reagan era, a prosperous and hopeful time in much of the country. You'd have thought that living in a flourishing and peaceful land would have fostered in adults an interest in teaching children the fundamentals of the market economy. In fact, it was the opposite. Adults weren't any more interested in talking about economics than I was in hearing about it. The only economics on offer came delivered in the oddly wrapped curricular package labeled "social studies"—a pre-woke bouillabaisse of history, criticism, theory, and popular nonsense about the shortcomings of market capitalism.

What is capitalism? The word gets bandied about a lot. How many people have a firm handle on what it really means? Merriam-Webster describes capitalism as "an economic system," and it's easy to see why they do—part of a dictionary's job is to keep up with how words are used and understood in real life. But that makes it sound as if capitalism were manufactured on purpose in a factory somewhere and maintained by a set of trained mechanics. It wasn't and it isn't.

The root is *capital*, a word with many possible meanings that in this case, as my succinct colleague Barton Swaim put it in a 2019 *Wall Street Journal* op-ed, refers to "money used to invest or build and so earn more money." Capitalism, therefore, could refer to a number of things. Some nouns ending with the suffix "-ism" relate to theories or ideas: conservatism, liberalism, feminism, regionalism. Often these theories or ideas have political consequences. Other nouns ending with "-ism" describe states of being: A person need not be an active drinker to suffer from alcoholism, for instance. The best definition of capitalism, I contend, is that capitalism is what capitalists do—it is the sum total of the actions of those private entrepreneurs who use money to invest or build so they can earn more money. That's capitalism. Add up all the investing and building of all the capitalists in a free market and you'll get something that resembles a "system." It looks to have been constructed and maintained but is in fact what the Austrian economist Friedrich Hayek called a "spontaneous order." Everyone is tending their own garden. It's completely voluntary. "The system" is merely a *summa* of individual choices and voluntary market transactions. No one manages or controls it. No one could.

A socialist economy, on the other hand, is a system for sure. The government, not private actors, decides how to invest and what to build. Participation is, for the most part, not voluntary. Social*ism* is what social*ists* do—they make plans. A socialist economy "must be created, planned, vigilantly monitored and forcefully regulated in order to function," Swaim notes. "But a market economy has no plan." In the words of the 18th-century Scottish philosopher Adam Ferguson, capitalism operating in a free market may look like a man-made mechanism. In fact, it is "the result of human action, but not the execution of any human design."

In my high school we never even got the dictionary definition of capitalism. Instead we learned about the economic inequality of the Gilded Age—Andrew Carnegie and Pittsburgh smog, John D. Rockefeller and the monopoly of

Standard Oil. Even if we didn't understand what free silver was in practical terms, we knew that William Jennings Bryan viewed it as a matter of economic justice for the little guy. Teddy Roosevelt was a hero for busting the trusts. We read about the horrors of the meatpacking industry. We met Samuel Gompers, Eugene V. Debs, and the fantastic populist figment called Tom Joad. We imbibed the unchallengeable assumption that wild speculation on unregulated stock markets was solely responsible for the misery of the Great Depression. Franklin Roosevelt tamed the animal spirits of the rapacious capitalists and didn't mind being tarred as a traitor to his class for his troubles. Only the blizzard of government spending required to mobilize a vast continental nation to fight a world war could breathe life into an economy that had been throttled to the brink of death by those who worship at the altar of the almighty Dow.

All of this was predicated on the assumption, still so popular, that economic growth is a zero-sum game. If John D. Rockefeller gets a piece of the pie, it means you can't have one. The rich get rich on the backs of the poor. Capitalism is fundamentally exploitative. In the United States at least, this is demonstrably untrue. The poorest American in 2022 is hundreds of times wealthier in real terms than the wealthiest American in 1776. He has greater access to essentials, like good food and quality housing, and enjoys a life expectancy that is essentially double what it was at the founding of the country. Rising societal wealth has financed medical and technical marvels that would have made Benjamin Franklin let go of his kite and stay in his bath for a week. You don't have to be an economic historian or a Nobel Prize winner to understand how far humanity has come; just look at the footwear. The Minute Men and milkmaids of the Revolutionary era would have killed to get their hands on a pair of cheap, durable, comfortable, stylish, and, most of all, easily replaceable Nike sneakers.

What free market capitalism has done for this country—and others—is nothing short of a miracle. Our ancestors, if they could see us, would be amazed by our wealth and comfort. And yet most teenagers graduate high school with only the dimmest impression of what markets are and how they work. The first economics most teenagers learn is the economics of celebrity. From watching the careers of their favorite athletes, movie stars, and musicians, a simple reality becomes clear: Famous people get rich. The surest route to material wealth is to be blessed with physical attractiveness or an outsized talent in a profession with the means to compensate you for it. So for most kids, the most salient economic question isn't "What do you want to do with your life and how can you organize your life to achieve those goals?" Rather it is "How does a person get famous?" Because if you can get famous, then you can get rich, and once you have one or the other of those things, life is candy.

It's lamentable that celebrity is the entry point to economics for so many of us. Before we know anything about how a household works, before we understand what our parents do for a living and how it relates to our general welfare, before we ever hear the words "supply" and "demand" spoken by someone who knows why they matter, we know that Leonardo DiCaprio makes $35 million per movie and that some kid from Indiana became a billionaire by making videos on TikTok. Things would be so much better if this distorted world view could be interrupted before taking hold in young minds and replaced with some real talk about trade-offs, incentives, choice, and competition. That's probably asking too much of our educational system at this point, but it isn't too much to ask of this book. I think schools should teach economics—the real kind, not fairy tales about lottery winners, movie stars, and athletes, and not horror stories about monocled, wealth-hoarding Monopoly men. Kids can handle the real stuff. It's not nearly as complicated as most credentialed economists insist on making it. Start from the start.

The Virtuous Cycle

Hesiod, a contemporary of Homer, may have been the first economist. His 828-verse poem "Works and Days," written about 700 BC, is full of advice on all manner of human problems. Some, it must be said, were problems specific to the ancient world: "Never pour a libation of sparkling wine to Zeus after dawn with unwashed hands." I am not in a position to say Hesiod is wrong about this. He also had some rather un-politically correct ideas about courtship. "Do not let a flaunting woman coax and cozen and deceive you: She is after your barn." Thanks, Hess. Good to know.

Hesiod may have been hopelessly old school, but there's no denying that his fundamental understanding of how to live a good life was sound. "Proportion is best in all things," he insists. Can't argue with that. He also apparently understood the importance of healthy competition, a very modern economic concept. "Neighbor vies with neighbor as he hurries after wealth . . . [and] this strife is wholesome for men." We can assume that keeping pace with A-listers like Homer motivated Hesiod to sharpen his pencil and knock out some self-imposed minimum of publishable verse every day. As a career, didactic poetry has never been a sure thing. "Potter envies potter, carpenter envies carpenter, beggar envies beggar, singer envies singer." All that stuff is still true, and anyone who's ever been close friends with someone in their own profession and at roughly the same stage of career understands the sentiment. Envy is a great motivator. Sometimes that little push you need in life comes from your own sense of keeping pace with the competition.

The fact of the matter is that in the 21st century we get out of our beds most mornings for reasons resembling those that have motivated humans throughout history. Not because we seek to grind our enemies into dust and not by an unrelenting desire for fame. Most of us are quite content with the general outlines of our lot in life, though small improvements are always welcomed at the margins. Similarly, we aren't pushed along through life by vague charitable impulses to do good for society. We are mainly, ✓ if not exclusively, interested in taking care of ourselves. We have bills to pay and mouths to feed. Hesiod and Homer did too. I guarantee it.

We rise and shine because we need a paycheck. If you are the type of person who gets out of bed every morning thinking solely about what you can do that day to make the world a better place, you probably have already achieved a level of material comfort that most of us can only dream about. That's good for you but it doesn't change the reality—people need to earn their own livings. The funny thing is, our combined efforts *do* make society better. We take those paychecks and spend them at the local movie theater, the neighborhood bar, the drugstore, the barbershop, and the supermarket. We throw the kid next door $20 to rake the leaves in the yard, which allows him to save up for that new racer hanging in the window down at the bicycle shop. All of this hand-to-hand commerce and industry gets the blood flowing in the local economy, helping our neighbors to pay their own bills and generating even more economic activity as the cycle repeats and compounds, and compounds again, presuming no agenda-driven meddlers try to interrupt it, generating ever more material well-being in a virtuous upward gusher of prosperity.

That's not all. Part of our income goes to the local government in the form of taxes, which pay the salaries of the teachers in our community and employ police, firefighters, and sanitation workers, who play their own part in making the local economy work. Another part of our income goes to the national government to pay for the big stuff, like the military, the interstate highways, and a few other pricey items. Government is notorious for waste and inefficiency, but educating children, keeping the streets safe and clean, and protecting the country from invasion are social goods that can't be written off. We need government and it can't pay for itself. A productive private economy operating under free market conditions generates new wealth for those who participate in it and kicks off taxes to fund the good things that government does. We'll come back to a fuller discussion of the relationship between the government and the market later.

If we're doing well, basic needs covered, we may also put some portion of our pay into a savings account at the bank, which turns around and lends it out to help people buy houses and start new businesses—a virtuous cycle of its own. We give some to a charity or church, which need cash to help those who can't help themselves to get back on their feet. Perhaps we stash some of what we earn in a retirement account that is invested in the global financial economy. Financial markets help allocate capital quickly and efficiently and direct society's accumulated wealth to productive uses. Entrepreneurs start new companies that make products and provide services that help solve problems in your neighborhood, on your street, in your house, in your life. They get money to start those companies from banks, maybe from the very same one where you have an account and into which you deposited part of your paycheck.

It's more than a virtuous cycle; it's a well-lubricated and responsive machine that provides people with access to the goods and services that they need and want—the ones they *actually* need and they *actually* want, not what some nanny-state bean counter or petty bureaucrat thinks they need and want. It allows people the opportunity to pursue the vocations and careers that suit them and the freedom to pursue their dreams. And all of it begins not with some desire on your part to buy the world a Coke or some hazy commitment to an indefinable notion of what's best for society, but with you getting up and going to work for your own selfish reasons. You certainly didn't do it to pay a cop's salary or finance some dreamer's risky venture. You went to work to take care of yourself—in pursuit of your own interests. It sounds strange to put it this way, but your "selfishness" set the whole thing in motion. It was the first domino to fall. It set off an economic chain of reactions leading to good outcomes running all the way to the horizon in every direction. The knock-on effects of your decision to go to work in the morning are too numerous even to imagine, much less to count. Now multiply that across the entire economy and you see what Adam Smith is talking about.

All of our selfish buzzing and scurrying adds up to something bigger. It moves the world forward in a way that we could never achieve if we woke up every day trying to figure out a way to move the world forward. That's the invisible hand, not some big foam finger pushing you into the mall. Greed isn't good, ambition is—ambition to improve your circumstances, ambition to feed yourself and your family, ambition to make a better life for the next generation. The free market is the only economic "system" that gives personal ambition a blue sky toward which to run.

It's my contention that Adam Smith only used the invisible hand metaphor once because he didn't think that the magical forces he was describing actually were impossible to see. He could see them, obviously, or he wouldn't have written *The Wealth of Nations*. You can see them too, if you know where to look. You see them every day.

When you choose to do the school play instead of going out for the baseball team, you see those magical forces. When you choose one gas station over another because of a slight difference in the price of regular unleaded, you see them. When you decide to skip a night out so you can wake up early and go to the gym, you see them. Once you cotton on to how prices are set and what they mean, once you realize that you live in an environment of scarcity and that this forces you to weigh trade-offs and make decisions at the margin, once you learn to look at the world the way Adam Smith did, the magical forces at work in the free market seem entirely visible.

In fact, you start seeing them everywhere.

CHAPTER 2

MARKETS

Markets have always been with us. Before there was cash money, before there was agriculture, before there was a written record, probably even before there was anything resembling law and a legal system, there was trade, and trade—this for that—is what makes a market. In caveman days, the guy in the tribe who had more nuts and berries than his family needed sought out the guy in the tribe who had more warm furs than his family needed. Those two guys, if they could find each other, agreed to terms and made a swap. This many nuts and berries for that many furs. Done deal. Nice doing business with you.

That swap was a particular form of trade called barter. No cash changed hands because no cash existed. But it was a market transaction, a voluntary and mutually beneficial exchange between two parties, each of whom needed something that the other had and was willing to give up something of value in their own possession to get it. Nobody was forced into the furs for nuts and berries deal. Nobody felt they were getting ripped off. Both sides walked away satisfied because both sides got what they wanted on terms they found fair. If either of them had felt that the trade was lopsided or rigged against them, they wouldn't have agreed to it in the first place. That's what truly free markets do—they satisfy people's needs and allocate resources fairly, efficiently, and without coercion.

Barter still happens all the time, often after school and on playgrounds. In the adult world, however, it isn't always easy to find a trading partner with whom to barter. Market information in a barter economy can be frustratingly scarce, although this is often by design. You don't want to risk getting clubbed over the head by a gang of knuckle-dragging thugs because you make the mistake of walking around advertising your overabundance of nuts and berries. But the main problem is finding someone who is actually looking to pick up some nuts and berries and who also happens to be in a position to supply the furs that appeal to you. This hard-to-arrange "double coincidence" makes barter an inefficient basis for an economy. Maybe your ideal trading partner won't be swinging by your cave for another six months. Maybe he crosses paths with another nut-and-berry man en route to your place and unloads all his precious furs before you even get a look at them. Where will you be then? When it comes to feeding and clothing your family, you don't want to leave things to chance—or barter.

A better basis for organizing an economy involves a stable and recognized medium of exchange—something that holds its value (unlike nuts and berries, which grow stale or go bad) and can be traded for all manner of goods (unlike furs, which offend some people). Anything with such properties is rightly called money, but it doesn't have to come in the form of a silver coin or a piece of paper currency. Cash is king these days, but gold, arrowheads, cigarettes, and cowrie shells have all served a similar purpose at certain times and in certain places. Modern economic history has been bought and paid for using fiat money, that which holds value because a governmental authority says so and serves as a medium of exchange because a government authority allows it to, but in our brave new world it isn't impossible to imagine the abolition of cash and the triumph of some sort of digital currency. Money will always be money. Currency is merely a form of money that everyone agrees on.

As a market transaction, nuts and berries for warm furs is only really different from an eBay auction, a real estate deal, or a modern securities contract in the fine print. Things can always get complicated, but the essentials are the same. You satisfy my need; I satisfy yours; everybody goes home happy. Add up all the little trades and side deals that people and businesses make every day and—*voilà!*—you've got yourself a market. Keep the siphoneers and chiselers out of it and you may actually get yourself a well-functioning market.

While markets have always been with us, they haven't always been free. Kings, potentates, monopolists, cheaters, bullies, and, notably, the radical followers of a misguided 19th-century German freeloader (whose last name is a four-letter word rhyming with *narcs*) have worked assiduously throughout history to inhibit voluntary exchange in markets of every type. Sometimes they do it for reasons of greed—everybody wants to get their beak wet. Sometimes they do it because they read a lot of garbage in college. Almost always they operate from a position of ignorance about the power of free markets to make people's lives better by lifting them out of poverty, giving them access to food and shelter, cleaning the air they breathe and the water they drink, curing the diseases that kill them, and providing them opportunities to put their talents to work in productive and satisfying ways. The best part is that all these things are accomplished by people acting not out of some selfless desire to make the world a better place but in what you might call the selfish pursuit of their own interests. That's the miracle of the market.

Free markets have other virtues. They go well with democracy, and democracies almost never go to war with each other, so hippies should support free markets for the same reasons that the chamber of commerce does. Free markets sing in perfect harmony with political liberty, allowing all people the space to create, compete, and cooperate in such ways as they see fit. Liberty has always been a somewhat suspect concept on the far left, and it has lately become a dirty word in some corners of the American right, but without it—and without a political class that values and protects it—tyranny is always just a madman away. Free markets make it hard for any one person or enterprise to accrue too much political power. When economic power is dispersed, political power tends to disperse as well. Economic freedom breeds political freedom and keeps power-hungry dingbats at bay. Dictators hate free markets because markets don't always do what they're told. They only obey the laws of supply and demand.

That's not to say that markets have always been perfect or ever could be perfect. In the short run, market competition produces winners and losers. In the long run, however, free markets are fair markets. They raise living standards for everyone in society. Then again, as a famous economist once said, in the long run we'll all be dead.

Markets have been known to fail—and to fail spectacularly. Sometimes in the process of working their magic they produce bad side effects like pollution or wasted resources. Economists, especially the credentialed variety, have occasionally been blind to the real human damage that some markets, functioning as they are supposed to, can cause to hardworking people and bystanders who have done nothing wrong. But an approach to economics that recognizes the unrivaled ability of sometimes chaotic free markets to improve people's material circumstances, at both the individual and societal levels, is clearly better for human flourishing than one that drags the whole ship down by trying to avoid all that mess through central planning.

It's not like we haven't been running this experiment for centuries. The data are in. Free markets, for all their faults, beat the pants off unfree markets. The cool thing is that markets usually insist on being free. When they are interfered with—when political actors attempt to restrain or restrict them—markets find a way to operate, either in the shadows as "black markets" or in another jurisdiction entirely. Markets are adaptable. Markets are mobile. Like water, they find their level.

The Fine Art of Household Management

Economics has also been with us a long time, though not quite as long as markets. The ancient Greeks called it *oikonomia* or, roughly translated, "household management." The modern mind goes immediately to home economics, that venerable high school class where generations of American teenagers learned to bake a tray of chocolate cupcakes and balance a simple checkbook. Bound up as it was with crusty midcentury assumptions about gender roles, home economics has fallen out of fashion, both as a matter of secondary education and as a guide for organizing our lives. Maybe it's for the best. Something tells me kids don't have much interest anymore in ironing the perfect crease into a trouser leg. It isn't hard to imagine a 21st-century home economics curriculum that revolves around optimizing the performance of the digital household. Unit 1: Select a username.

The French picked up the word at some point, as *économie*, and it began to acquire some secondary meanings having to do with frugality and thrift. An "economical" person makes the most of what he has. How? By making smart choices about the trade-offs he faces. Economizing, or living economically, is not the prevailing ethos of our time. We have graduated from the age of thrift and delayed gratification. We live now in the age of the quick hit and debt-fueled consumption. The days of the sewing machine are over; these are the days of free shipping and free returns. Some would say this is evidence of capitalism's corrosive effects on a culture over time. They wouldn't be entirely wrong, but they wouldn't be entirely correct, either. If a society can hear the unmistakable sound of what the mid-20th-century Austrian economist Joseph Schumpeter called the "perennial gale of creative destruction," then it can be pretty sure its markets are working as intended. Products and services become wildly popular, entrepreneurs rush to provide them, then tastes change as new products and new services become wildly popular. Industries come and industries go. Companies emerge as upstarts before they refine their offerings and make themselves competitive. They topple established players that have grown bloated and inefficient. Then they try to stay lean and reactive to their customers' needs lest they become targets for the next generation of upstarts. In societies where bureaucratic busybodies direct production and regulate consumption, the sewing machine is still very much in everyday use, though the indicators of human flourishing flatlined long ago.

One can only wonder what went into managing a Greek household in, say, 500 BC. Getting the kids to keep their dirty togas off the floor was probably as difficult then as it is today. But while your average Athenian didn't have empty calories and bounced checks to worry about, household management hasn't changed as much as you might think in 2,500 years. Every household still needs to bring in enough income to cover expenses, maybe with a little left over for a jug of nice retsina at the weekend. Household management is about so much more than balancing the books. The ancient Greeks excelled at many things, among which was observing the world they lived in. They had a knack for examining their own quirks and saying, "Why do we do things the way we do?" They were logical, self-reflective, and self-critical. In a good way. While other ancient peoples tended to think their life circumstances were dictated by the whims of gods and goddesses in the astral plane, the Greeks were inclined to use human reason in the here and now to analyze and systematize their own behavior and, if necessary, make smart changes.

"Yo, Timon, when you gonna start living within your means?"

The ancient Greeks were not economists in the modern sense. They wouldn't have recognized most of the concepts we ascribe to the discipline now. There was no supply and demand discussed in the gymnasia—not explicitly, anyway. Those magical forces were present but undiscovered, ghostly influences moving undetected and unremarked upon in the places where goods were sold, services offered, and contracts of exchange negotiated and signed. It would be a long time before the economics that we recognize as economics would have its day in the sun.

Economics is how we make sense of markets. It's the study of how voluntary transactions work, humanity's attempt at grasping the dynamics at play in the markets where we buy, sell, and trade so that we can better understand our own interests and behavior, given the limitations we all face. Not all market transactions are financial; in fact, most aren't. Many don't even involve a material exchange of money, goods, or services. Ultimately, economics is our guide to making better choices and smarter decisions. It isn't a man-made phenomenon, some kind of Rube Goldberg machine cooked up by bankers and stockbrokers. It's also not a system of political control or a vehicle for exploitation. It's not accounting. It's not inequality. It's not greed. It's not gross domestic product, and it's not the unemployment rate. Economics is what ivory tower types call a social science—some, in fact, call it the *queen* of the social sciences—which is a way of saying it's neither a science nor an art. It falls somewhere in between. There are elements of economics that can be quantified and systematized and studied like a hard science, and there are elements of economics that are best understood without resort to numbers, charts, and graphs. I'm a words man, myself, so I gravitate toward the non-numerical. Let me tell you a story.

Mr. Seaver's Mural

Mr. Seaver was my junior high school science teacher. A big, barrel-chested guy with a voice like a foghorn, Mr. Seaver was also the boys' soccer coach. He had a well-deserved reputation among students as a hard-ass. I don't know where he was from or how he ended up teaching in a junior high school in suburban New Jersey in the mid-'80s, but Mr. Seaver didn't mess around, either in the classroom or on the playing field. He would regularly challenge the guys on the soccer team to leg-lift endurance competitions so he could show off just how strong his abdominal muscles were, even in middle age. We were 13. He was convinced, wrongly (I think?), that thick, rippling abs were the key to success in soccer. I don't know. Maybe he was right. I'm sure they don't hurt.

Mr. Seaver was old school. Any boy caught in the hallway wearing a baseball hat could expect the kind of sweaty-faced dressing down that drill instructors give new Marines on Parris Island. While I was determined to avoid the guy pretty much at all times, it wasn't always possible. I was on the soccer team, after all, and he was my science teacher. I definitely remember his lessons on what seem to me now like marginally scientific things, such as subliminal advertising, and I absolutely dissected a formaldehyde-preserved frog on one of his lab tables, but I managed to keep a lowish profile and was spared the full brunt of his notorious wrath.

In my eighth-grade year, my locker was situated directly across the way from Mr. Seaver's classroom. One morning, as I was unloading my bookbag, he appeared in the hallway toting a stepladder. From a large leather tote that looked like Johnny Appleseed's spare satchel, he pulled a stencil set, pencils, a few rags, and a small pot of black paint. Balancing his tools as he climbed the ladder, Mr. Seaver proceeded to trace out an inscription in the harshly lit wall space between the top of the lockers and the drop ceiling. The halls filled with curious teenagers, most of whom weren't on the soccer team and so had never lost a leg-lift competition to him. We watched as he worked. The words began to take shape on the wall.

Life is not determined by what you want. Life is determined by the choices you make.

It seemed to me a message somewhat at odds with Mr. Seaver's style, which could best be described as let's-get-in-there-and-blow-their-doors-off. On the face of it, this was the sort of sticky, meaningless sentiment you'd expect a Hallmark card writer to reject. But I was transfixed. The message was unlike any that I'd theretofore been asked to consider. One brave non-soccer player emerged from the crowd.

"Hey Mr. Seaver," he said. "What are you doing all that up there for?" The hallways at my junior high school were otherwise free of inspirational inscriptions. Mr. Seaver paused as he carefully wiped down his paintbrushes and began replacing the tools in his satchel.

"I'm giving you guys the best advice you're ever gonna get, that's what I'm doing," he said quietly, his eyes focused on the clean-up job. "And I'm writing it on the wall so you see it every day. Maybe then you won't forget it."

Life is not determined by what you want. Life is determined by the choices you make.

I took it all in, wondering whether he was right, both on the merits of the adage and on the question of whether I'd forget. About the only choice I had to make that particular afternoon was whether to go straight home after school or stop off at the corner store to buy some potato chips and cream soda to share with my friends while shooting hoops in the driveway. I pocketed Mr. Seaver's little life lesson and went on about my teenage business. But every day that year and the next, as I passed through that hallway, I glanced up to see that stenciled slogan on the wall. And every day that I did, those words sunk like seeds into the rich, wet soil of my teenage soul. As I've gotten older I've learned, sometimes the hard way, that life really isn't determined by what you want. The choices you make may be informed by what you want, but the choice is really the only thing that counts. I've learned that lesson so many times by now that I couldn't forget it even if I wanted to. Mr. Seaver went two-for-two.

Mr. Seaver was a science teacher, but economics may have been his true vocation. I think he would agree that learning to look at decision-making the way an economist does can help you pull back the curtain on the hidden impulses and involuntary actions that move lives and, by extension, move politics, move businesses, move families, and move communities. People's behaviors are often motivated by economic concerns—not by money necessarily, but by an intuitive understanding that resources are scarce, trade-offs are necessary, and choices matter.

No matter who you are or where you live, you make all sorts of consequential choices every day. They can be big or they can be small. When you find yourself deciding whether to drop out of college and take a job, you may be intensely aware that the choice you make could alter the ultimate direction of your life. The stakes may be somewhat lower when you're weighing whether to let your Netflix subscription expire so you can save a few bucks every month, but the difference is not as big as you suppose. It's a matter of degree. Even when you elect to put off a decision until sometime in the future, you are behaving like an economist. Not to choose is still to make a choice.

You Can't Always Get What You Want

At its heart, economics is about choice. Sometimes academic economists and professors like to take it a little further and say that economics is about choice in an environment of scarcity. All that means is that most of the time we have to choose among options that aren't perfect, or even all that great. Scarcity implies limits, and the world we live in is full of them—physical limits, mental limits, limits on what we can consume, limits on what we can spend, limits on what we can save, limits on how high we can jump. If you're in the mood for a nice bottle of wine, you might be limited by how much cash you have in your wallet. If you're in the market for a new home, you might be limited by the amount of money you've set aside for a down payment and the amount of credit a bank will be willing to offer you. If you're looking for a new job, you might be limited by the number of available positions, the salaries on offer, and the quality of your résumé. If you're hunting for a spouse, you might be limited by the personal qualities you yourself bring to the table—that is, by what you see in the mirror.

Without these limits you wouldn't have to make any choices. You could pick any bottle of wine that suited your fancy, regardless of price. You could walk into the bank and tell them you wanted a loan to buy the most expensive house in town, whether or not you had the down payment or the means to afford the mortgage payments. You could work at any job that appealed to you and date anybody in town. If you lived in an environment of plenty rather than an environment of scarcity, the laws of economics might not apply to you. But you do live in such an environment, and the laws do apply. They apply to all of us. The simple fact governing everything we do in life is this: We can't have everything we want. And if we want something, we almost always have to give up something we value to get it. This idea sits at the center of classical economics.

In "Works and Days," Hesiod outlined the difficulties of a life lived in an environment of scarcity. This has always been the human condition, and Hesiod understood it well. He was born into an agrarian world of subsistence farmers who scraped a living out of the cold, hard ground. The value of a person's labor was reflected in what showed up on the dinner table every night: "Do not put your work off till tomorrow and the day after; for a sluggish worker does not fill his barn." If you want to eat, and maybe to set aside a little something for the family's future, then sloth just ain't going to get the job done. Good things may come to those who wait, but not to those who refuse to work while they wait. Pulling on your boots and putting in the hours is the only way forward. He compares the lazy man to "the stingless drones who waste the labor of the bees, eating without working."

"Work is no disgrace," Hesiod says bluntly. "It is idleness which is a disgrace."

If that view seems harsh, recall that the ancient world could be a brutal place, especially if you were frail, vulnerable, sick, or disabled. Hesiod was simply calling it as he saw it. You may not want to get up and get after it, you may not want to study late into the night, you may not want to live in a world where your choices are constrained by limits beyond your control. But life is not determined by what you want. Life is determined by the choices you make.

CHAPTER 3

MOTIVATIONS

In the winter of 1996–97 you couldn't turn on the TV or the radio for five minutes without hearing someone shout, "Show me the money." It was the catchphrase of the moment, drawn from the smash Tom Cruise romantic comedy *Jerry Maguire*. People said it in stores, at Christmas parties, when they were cashing their paychecks, and when they were getting change from a gas station attendant. Like "Where's the beef?" and "Who let the dogs out?," it was one of those unavoidable cultural touchpoints that penetrate the national consciousness so deeply that you find yourself begging for it to please go away—a meme before memes.

Jerry Maguire is the story of a man who realized that true happiness would remain out of reach so long as his life revolved around that thing Cuba Gooding Jr.'s character kept asking to be shown. "For the love of money is the root of all evils," as the Bible says. Some seem to think economics is about money. If that were true, actors, athletes, and rock stars would rank among our top economists. They have been economically successful, in the sense that they found a way to combine what talents God gave them—aka their "resource allocation"—and use them to make lots of money. But economics isn't about making money; it's about making choices. And while many economic choices involve money, many do not. Maybe even most do not.

The economist's view of life requires knowing what you want and figuring out how to get it. Usually that means figuring out the thing (or things) of value you will have to give up to get the thing (or things) you want. Sometimes that's money. Most of the time it's not. "Getting the most out of life means choosing wisely and well," writes economist and podcast talker Russ Roberts in his 2014 book *How Adam Smith Can Change Your Life*. "And making choices—being aware of how choosing one road means not taking another, being aware of how my choices interact with the choices of others—that's the essence of economics." The very concept of making a choice presupposes the existence of possibilities. To choose one option is to forgo others. Remember, we live in an environment of scarcity, which means that even when we have the opportunity to choose among options, we can't have them all. There are limits. When we decide to exercise one option we are necessarily giving up some other option (or options). That may sound like common sense, but it's actually a big deal and the knowledge of it has momentous consequences.

Knowing what you want is one thing. Knowing what you stand to lose out on if you get what you want is another level entirely.

The Centrality of Choice

If economics is about choice, how should we think about choice? It's possible to conceive of choice as a positive action—when you buy a comic book, you gain a comic book. It's equally possible to think of choice as a negative action—when you buy a comic book, you give up your allowance. Either way you can't have both your allowance and the comic book. That option is ruled out. But if you choose the second option, to give up your allowance and buy the comic book, you also give up something that economists put a great deal of emphasis on: the freedom to use your allowance to do something other than buy a comic book. If you think that buying a comic book is only a matter of money, then you're thinking like an accountant. Once you realize that it's also a matter of lost opportunity, then you're starting to think like an economist.

I mentioned in chapter 1 that I struggled with a time trade-off in high school between acting in the school play and going out for the baseball team. Now my oldest daughter is in high school and she's the one facing these tough trade-offs. Alongside the piles of homework and the never-ending social dramas looms the college question: Is she doing what she needs to do to help her get into college? We talk about it all the time. What sports should she play? Which clubs should she join? Can she do an after-school job? What about volunteer opportunities?

The dilemma is the same today as it was for me back in the 1980s. If she does that online Greek course that we think will look really good on her applications, there's no way she can also play for the school basketball team. Something's gotta give, and it won't be something that doesn't matter. Giving up basketball comes with a cost for her, just like giving up baseball and soccer came with a cost for me. If you can imagine trying to quantify the benefit of something like an online Greek course or a chance to play a starring role in a high school play, the cost of all forgone opportunities must be weighed.

Most of the time we do these kinds of calculations on the fly. You don't necessarily need to know what goes into the baking of a cupcake in a bakery to make an in-the-moment decision about whether it's worth purchasing at the posted price. Surely the baker himself keeps a running tally of how much he has invested in flour, sugar, butter, rent, gas to heat his oven, electricity to keep his lights on, and even his own education so he could learn to be a baker. All that stuff factors into the price tag he decides to put on his cupcake, but you don't need to consider all of that—or any of it—to know that while biting into that moist, delicious confection might suit your fancy in the here and now, it comes with a trade-off. Your resources are scarce, like everyone's, and if you overpay for the cupcake in the afternoon it may limit your options in the evening.

All this happens in the blink of an eye when you spy something delicious in the bakery window and see how much they want to charge you for it. You're a better economist than you think.

The decision to buy a cupcake or a comic book is far more straightforward than the decision to invest time and money in education, relationships, and social or cultural experiences. We rarely get out a pen and paper and start assigning numerical values to various options when the choice is between nursing school and a year on a fishing boat in Alaska. We do the math implicitly. We think on things. We consult with people we trust. We examine our options. Sometimes we react instinctively to the options we are presented with. Our desires (or our biases, if you can handle that word) are often buried deep within. We like something because we like it. We're drawn in a particular direction as if by invisible forces of attraction. Other times we really lay on the cost-benefit analysis. I wanted to play baseball in high school, but not nearly as much as I wanted to star in the school play. You may have wanted to taste that fancy cupcake at the overpriced bakery, but not quite enough to part with the $10 you had earmarked for a cab ride home after the movie that night. Ultimately, our preferences—what we value the most—are revealed by our choices.

A Bird in Hand

Businesses, like individuals, wrestle with trade-offs all day long. Pursuing certain opportunities means foreclosing on others. Investing in one area means neglecting another. A factory that expects a surge in orders must stock up on raw materials and hire extra workers to meet that expected demand. The possibility always exists that those orders may not materialize and the factory could end up stuck with a bunch of component parts it can't assemble into a finished product that it can sell and a bunch of workers who are getting paid to sit around doing nothing all day. But what if those orders do materialize? Well, if the penny-pinchers in the front office had tried to scrimp on the purchasing order or had only hired half as many workers as they needed to satisfy their customers, there would have to be a reckoning at some point. The prospective purchaser of those finished goods may see the writing on the wall and go somewhere else with his big order.

What's the right move for the factory manager? It's not always clear. You have to put your finger in the wind, and you have to weigh the trade-offs.

The same dynamic applies to small businesses. A restaurant that buys too much fresh produce and hamburger meat runs the risk of getting stuck with a bunch of spoiled food in its refrigerator if for some reason nobody shows up on Saturday night. The stakes are high; food, unlike nuts and bolts in a factory, goes bad—and sometimes it goes bad fast. Restaurants live on a knife-edge much of the time, worried that people won't go out to eat and all their fresh ingredients will go to waste. But what if instead of an empty restaurant, a bus pulls up on Saturday night filled with four hungry softball teams who just finished a daylong tournament and want to gorge on cheeseburgers with fresh lettuce and tomatoes? It would be a pity to have to turn them (and their money) away. The person in charge of stocking the pantry has to get real good, real quick at estimating what the kitchen staff is going to need and calculating the risk of getting it wrong. Throwing away too much spoiled food will sink the business eventually. Getting tagged with a reputation as the kind of place where the burgers are good but frequently out of stock could just as easily ruin the restaurateurs' dreams. Even figuring out what time to open a restaurant involves trade-offs. There's a cost associated with keeping the doors open and the lights on. That cost stings most when there aren't any paying customers at the tables to offset it.

Figuring out when to open and close takes trial and error. In fact, trial and error—searching for the right mix of risk and opportunity—plays a big part in the success of just about every business. Chance plays a part, too. Hamburgers can go out of fashion. Factories can find themselves making a product that nobody wants to buy anymore. That's why businesses need to be adaptable, and adaptability is about getting good at weighing the trade-offs.

My business is no exception to the iron rule that life is about trade-offs. I work as an editor in the opinion section of the *Wall Street Journal*. Space on our pages is extremely limited. We have room for four or five op-eds from outside contributors every day. When the news cycle is running hot, we can receive as many as 100 times that many submissions. The decision about what to put on the page and what to pass over has consequences. Many of the pieces we reject are worthy. Some will surely find a home with our competitors if we say no. Those op-eds may become widely read and talked about. They may even move policy, and we'll get none of the credit if and when they do.

This is a cost we have to consider when we decide not to run a piece. Our process is opaque. Unlike a new car rolling off an assembly line or a cheeseburger at a popular restaurant, the value of any particular op-ed is almost impossible to quantify. It may be well-written but on a topic that only three or four people in the country would consider interesting enough to read. It may be somewhat alluring conceptually but written at a third-grade level. It may come attached to a notable byline. It may be a great idea, sharply argued and sharply written, but the author may be someone with no recognized authority to opine on the subject in question. It could be a dream piece by the world's foremost expert offering a new perspective on a timely matter, but we may have run something on the same subject by somebody else the day before. It could be okay but too short, okay but too long. How to decide? What to do?

We do exactly what factory penny-pinchers and restaurant purchasing managers do. We use our professional judgment and weigh the trade-offs. My colleagues and I consider the merits of each piece along with our needs at that particular time and come to the conclusion that feels most right in the moment. It's not a science. Sometimes the deciding factor between two pieces is length. Does it fit the limited space we have available? Is it going to take us all afternoon trying to edit it down? Sometimes an objectively better piece gets passed over for a lesser piece that fits. That's rare, but we work on a deadline so it does happen. We go into every decision about every piece knowing that we are potentially giving up something of value, but there's only so much room in the paper. We can't publish it all.

Life is about trade-offs. Some trade-offs are more painful than others.

There are trade-offs that will break your heart. Imagine you're a carpenter. You get a call to come work on a job that's going to require a six-month commitment. The money isn't great, but you like the fact that it's guaranteed work for a fixed period of time. It's rare to book out your calendar for a solid six months. That matters. As a carpenter, you don't always have the luxury of knowing where next month's paycheck is going to come from, so you're enthusiastic about the job offer. You're waffling a little, though, because you can't help worrying that something better might come along, something that promises more pay for less work—or better work. You decide to stall for a few days, hoping that if something more appealing is coming along it does so quickly. After 24 hours you start to get the sense that the six-month job is in danger of slipping away, so you call up the contractor who offered it to you and tell him you can start right away.

One thing we've known since caveman days is that it's better to have something now than that same thing in the future. Aretha Franklin wouldn't sing until she'd been paid, up front and in cash; she'd been burned too many times by promoters who disappeared after the show. A restaurant doesn't want to wait until Saturday night to see if they can fill their dining room; they want a fully booked-out reservation list on Saturday morning. Most carpenters would rather have a guaranteed gig right now, even if it pays slightly less, than a promise of that same gig in the future. So much can happen between now and then, between today and tomorrow. The certainty of having a thing now is worth something. You can put a dollar value on it. Unless you—our imaginary carpenter—have some real information on a big opportunity coming down the pike, chances are good that you'll take the guaranteed six months of relatively low-paid work rather than sit around waiting for something better to come along.

But wouldn't you know it? Not three days into the job you get the call you were hoping to get, offering you the same amount the six-month job is paying you for half the time commitment. It's the worst feeling in the world to have to turn a remunerative opportunity down because you've already said yes to something else. If you had it to do over again you might make a different choice, but you never—or rarely—have it to do over again. Most of the time you have to make difficult decisions with limited information. You are guided by the knowledge that you live in an environment of scarcity; that a thing now is worth more than that same thing later; that life is about trade-offs. Sometimes you've just got to pull the trigger.

Two in the Bush

What economists call "opportunity cost"—the lost potential gain from giving up one option for another—is intimately bound up with the idea of living in a world of trade-offs. Because we can't always get what we want, we are often forced to choose from a menu of bad options and worse options. The difference between minimizing the downside and maximizing the upside of any particular situation is a matter of perspective. When Taylor Swift schedules a concert in Houston on a particular night, she gets paid a considerable fee. What does she give up? Her time and energy, certainly, and whatever costs in terms of labor, permitting, travel, and so on are involved with taking a concert tour on the road. But she also gives up the freedom to play a show in New York City on that same night for what might have been a higher fee. The difference, if there is one, between what Taylor could make for playing at Madison Square Garden and what she will make for playing at Houston's NRG Stadium must necessarily be part of her choice about where to play and when.

Now, Taylor may see some value in visiting her Houston fans once in a while, and it could be enough to even up the financial score with the payday she'd see at Madison Square Garden, but just like me when I was in high school, and just like you—the imaginary carpenter—she can't be in two places at once. The rules are the rules.

So where should Taylor play? If she can make a higher fee in New York on a given night then it seems logical that she should play there and not in Houston or any other city. Indeed, a lot of artists choose to do just that. The Las Vegas nightlife economy is almost entirely based on this idea—performers spare themselves the costs associated with putting a show on the road by taking up residency in one spot. The audience comes to them. But Taylor Swift may have other concerns besides the size of her paycheck. She can perhaps manage to shake down a promoter for a sky-high fee, but what if that promoter isn't able to sell out the arena? It could be embarrassing for her to play in front of a half-empty house. She's supposed to be the voice of her generation, right? At a certain point, even Taylor Swift can't avoid the effect of one of economics' most inflexible limitations: the law of diminishing returns. At a certain point, each additional show that she plays in a particular city will yield her less benefit than the one before it, either in terms of the money she earns or in other terms that matter to her and her team, such as looking foolish by overstaying their welcome. How long will it take? Two days? A week? A month? A year?

The question then becomes, how many shows should Taylor play in New York before hitting the road for Houston, Las Vegas, or some other city? The decision facing Taylor will be made, as economists like to say, at the margins. That is, it's not simply a matter of whether to play at Madison Square Garden. She will. Doing a concert in New York is obviously in Taylor's interest. But how much utility she derives from playing the next show, or the marginal one, is what matters most to her—or what should.

Anyone who's ever been in an exclusive relationship intuitively understands the concept of opportunity cost. Being attached to that one person makes you unavailable to the rest of the known universe of romantic partners. Going steady or getting married may come with great benefits, but there's always a price: You're off the market. Opportunity cost is the value—*to you*—of whatever it is you're missing out on.

Incentives Matter

No two people are totally alike. Everyone's an individual, unique and special. But when you really get down to the nitty-gritty, we aren't so different either. One of the key maxims of economics is that people respond to incentives. Humans have hopes and dreams, we have desires and preferences, but we are rational. We see the world as it is, for the most part, and evaluate what we see in light of what we define as our own best interest. Suppose I'm a 22-year-old who recently graduated from college. Further suppose that I've managed to line up a great entry-level job in my chosen profession. The pay isn't great, but it's the career path I've spent four long years studiously preparing to pursue, so I'm perfectly happy to get in on the ground floor and hustle for a while so I can build up my résumé and, hopefully, prove my value to the company. I'd also like to build up a little cash cushion before I head out into the big, bad world, so I decide to move back in with my parents for a few months. Not a big deal, right? Lots of young grads do it, and my parents don't seem to mind at all.

Things are going great with my little post-college savings plan, and before you know it a few months turn into six months, which turns into nine months. I'm loving my job and especially loving all the money I'm socking away in the bank. One day, totally out of nowhere, my mom busts into my room and says I better "think again, mister" if I'm planning to live here rent free forever while she does my laundry and restocks the cereal shelf. She says she didn't raise a "Minnie the Moocher," whatever the heck that's supposed to mean. Apparently she and my dad feel they have "held up their end of the bargain" by sending me to college and that "the gravy train is coming into the station." I have until the end of the month to find an apartment of my own or it'll be "time to start paying the piper," by which my mom means I'll have to sign a lease on my childhood bedroom.

I didn't fall off the turnip truck yesterday. I understand where my mom is coming from, but this turn of events puts a severe crimp in my post-grad plans. I had been counting on another six months at least of keeping my expenses at rock-bottom lows while I banked those paychecks and built up a nest egg to help fund my assault on the world. While I'm far from having a fortune, I'm actually getting close to being able to put a nice down payment on a small house. All of a sudden, however, there's a line in the sand. Mom thinks I've been getting "a free ride." Out of the blue I've got something resembling an incentive to grow up. It seems absurd to me to have to pony up to my parents every month just so I can continue to crash in my high school hang space, but I'm stuck. It's decision time. If I'm going to have to pay the piper anyway, maybe I should just get my own place. Then I think, nah, if I move out I'll have to shop for myself and find a place to do my laundry. Living at home is still worth it, I decide, even if I have to pay a little rent every month. My mother's ultimatum isn't enough to overcome my clear incentive to stay put and stay home.

"Get the lease," I say. "Show me where to sign."

Good story, right? Now, dig this: Not every incentive is created equal. Let's add a detour to this choose-your-own-adventure exercise. Turn back the clock to that first few months post-graduation where I'm living in my parents' house rent free and loving it. We're still a few months away from mom telling me I have to pay up or move out. For the sake of argument, let's say I meet a young lady at work and we really hit it off. One things leads to another, I ask her out, and she says yes. At some point during our first date she inquires coyly about my living setup. I figure honesty is the best policy, so I tell her about the setup with my childhood bedroom and how it's weird and totally not permanent but it's a sweet little deal because really saved a lot of money and there's no way I could find such a bargain on the open market. Up until that moment things had been going my way. I spoke; she listened. She spoke; I listened. We laughed at each other's jokes. We seemed to have a connection. But the change, when it came, was sharp and unmistakable. It happened in the space behind her eyes, that place where lies can't live. A light that had moments earlier been bright and engaged flickers quickly and goes dark. I recognize the look on her face: contempt. The tone of her voice betrays repulsion even as she tells me that she thinks my relationship with my parents is "so sweet" and that I'm probably "doing the smart thing by trying to save some money."

Everybody is motivated by something. It could be a desire to get rich; it could be a desire to accumulate power; it could be a desire for reputation; it could be a desire to live a quiet life. A lot of the time it's desire itself that motivates us. When faced with a set of choices, a rational person will consider the alternatives and respond to the incentives. He won't have to spend a whole lot of time examining his preferences because he'll already be pretty familiar with those. In the imaginary situation I've sketched out, the 22-year-old me was perfectly at peace with his preferences (living at home, saving money) until mom busted in and said I'd have to pay up or get out. But that incentive, financial in nature, wasn't enough to shift my preferences to the point that I thought it made sense to get my own place. I considered the opportunity costs, weighed the trade-offs, and decided to stay put. On the other hand, when that pretty girl looked at me like I was the most pathetic creature in her universe, things shifted in a hurry. Suddenly I had a non-financial incentive to launch out of my childhood bedroom, and it actually led me to reorder my preferences. They say money makes the world go round. In my experience there are one or two other factors that do as much or more of the spinning.

CHAPTER 4

PREFERENCES

A baseball manager likes to keep a certain type of player on the team. He's usually a smallish guy, not quite good enough as a hitter to make the starting lineup, but he's scrappy and doesn't mind waiting for an opportunity to contribute. He may not get to play every day, but when he does he almost always makes a difference. His real value to the manager stems from his versatility in the field. He can play any position, and usually he can play it well. He gets slotted in as circumstances dictate at third base, right field, or, in extra-innings games that have turned silly, as a last-gasp relief pitcher, making him at times more helpful to the manager than most of the other guys on the team, even if they are better in an all-around way at their particular positions than this player, who is frequently called a "utility man."

Theater companies and sailing ships have utility men and women on their rosters too. Businesses, sports teams, political campaigns, military regiments—enterprises with lots of people involved are comparable to machines with a lot of moving pieces. To keep them running smoothly you need a lot of replacement parts. Most parts are extremely specific. They can do one job and one job only. Some parts are adaptable; they are meant for one job but can be repurposed to do something else reasonably well. But it's good to have a reliable utility part, or a utility man, that you can plug into any open job in a pinch. A baseball manager loves to have a couple of guys in the lineup who can hit moonshot home runs, not to mention some contact specialists who can be relied on to put the ball in play, but those players are no good to him if they're hurt. If his best players go down for their count, the manager looks immediately for someone who can satisfy his needs. Sometimes I like to think of him as the world's most pedestrian superhero: "This looks like a job for Utility Man!"

In everyday parlance, utility means usefulness, or the quality of being able to put a thing to practical use. In economics, it also means that, though there's slightly more to economic utility than mere usefulness. Utility is both broader and more nuanced than usefulness. The utility man's job on a baseball team is to do not just what the manager wants him to do but what the manager needs him to do. When the manager is stuck, he turns to the utility man. That's a little different than being useful. Utility is more substantial than usefulness. It carries more weight.

Think of it this way: A hammer is useful, a handy thing to have around the house, but when the time comes to put a nail in the wall to hang a picture, a hammer demonstrates its utility in a way that transcends mere handiness. When a worker is doing his job and producing value for the company, he's providing utility in a way that he isn't when he's on lunch break. When he's off the clock, he's the same guy. Same skills. No utility. Economic utility is more like satisfaction than usefulness. A pen is a useful thing in the abstract, but using that pen to sign your name to an employment contract or a mortgage agreement is what provides the utility. Compared to a thing that satisfies your actual needs, a thing that is merely useful pales. Satisfaction produces happiness; usefulness, at least the way we typically understand the word, doesn't deliver quite as much. It's a fine distinction, perhaps, but you would do well to bear it in mind.

Democritus, a philosopher who lived around the time of Socrates, gets the credit for first identifying something that, while it seems obvious, has momentous implications: Not everybody likes the same things. A thing may mean more to one person than it does to another. The value that you or I assign to a pickup truck, a fancy haircut, or a restaurant meal is entirely subjective and will have an effect on how much we are willing to pay. If we expect to gain a lot of utility from an experience or the consumption or use of a particular good, if it satisfies our needs, then an economist would say we have assigned it some amount of economic utility. How you decide to measure utility is up to you. Sometimes it's possible to do it in dollar terms. More often you do it other ways.

To be human is to have preferences. Many of our preferences are hardwired into our brains at birth, or maybe even before. Some of them we pick up along the way as we grow and are exposed to new sensations and new experiences. Most of our preferences are rational; many are not. We may or may not know why we have a weakness for strawberry ice cream. We just like it, and when given the option between strawberry and chocolate, we usually go with the strawberry. Is that an economic decision? You bet it is. You made a choice. Your preferences led you to choose one option over another, and your choice revealed which flavor provided you with greater utility. Without even realizing it you assigned more utility to strawberry than you did to chocolate. This is one of those things that economists make very complicated, with equations and models and all sorts of academic disagreement over minutiae. It doesn't need to be complicated. It's as simple as it sounds. We all have preferences.

It's important to note that preferences aren't destiny. You have free will; you are perfectly at liberty to deny or defy your own preferences, or even to discard old preferences and adopt new ones. Preferences can and do change, often as a result of experimentation that an economics of pure rationality might not predict with much accuracy. Still, the notion of your individual preferences is extremely important because it gives us a starting point from which we can begin to answer certain basic economic questions.

The Finest of the Flavors

I'm glad somebody brought up strawberry ice cream. I like it. Always have. But what is the value, to me, of a thing like strawberry ice cream? I mean, really. Most places you go to buy ice cream will offer a scoop of chocolate and a scoop of strawberry for exactly the same price. From that point of view, they are interchangeable, as are all the other flavors available to choose from. They're all ice cream. How bad could they be? How can I, or anyone, possibly assign an objective value to my preference for strawberry over chocolate? The answer is vexing: I can't, at least not in a numerical or scientific way, yet somehow I do manage to have a preference. So do you. You do this stuff all the time. Most of the choices we make are done without a full pre-game accounting of the likely outcomes, but our choices are themselves an expression of the value we place (or don't) on various things. Your choices reveal your preferences.

My preference for strawberry over chocolate exists; it has a value even if I don't know what it is or how to express it, apart from destroying two scoops with sprinkles in a waffle cone. If all other considerations are the same, I will usually choose strawberry over chocolate every time because of its utility to me. Where things get tricky is when all other considerations aren't the same, so let's do a little thought experiment.

Let's say you are like me and you love strawberry ice cream. All things being equal you will always choose the strawberry over another flavor. In most ice cream shoppes the options are priced by the number of scoops, not the type of flavor, so we can think of chocolate, strawberry, and rocky road as essentially substitutes for one another. But what if I told you that in this particular shoppe into which you've wandered, a scoop of chocolate costs $1 but a scoop of strawberry costs $100? That's a pretty big price difference—I'm guessing it would be more than enough to change your mind about which flavor you'd select. Welcome to Chocolate City. Note, however, that the extreme price differential doesn't change your mind about which flavor you prefer. All things being equal, you'd rather have strawberry. But all things aren't equal anymore. When it comes to price, a scoop of one flavor is no longer the same as a scoop of another.

Still, let's hold on a second. Before you settle for a cheap scoop of chocolate ice cream you don't really want, let me explain something to you. Prices aren't arbitrary things. They reflect a host of real considerations including, in the case of strawberry ice cream, the cost, quality, and provenance of the ingredients. So what if I explained that anyone who truly loves strawberry ice cream, who really considers himself a connoisseur, has to taste this particular strawberry ice cream in this particular shoppe. Why? Because it is made from the rarest and most intensely flavored strawberries, grown in the French countryside by a family that converted its black pinot noir vineyard in the Champagne region to a strawberry patch in 1952 and has previously only allowed its fruit to be sold to the French Ministry of Foreign Affairs for use in desserts served at black-tie dinners given for the world's diplomats. Would that move the needle? I'll tell you something else: The cream this stuff is made from comes from a herd of Montbéliarde cattle that are the only dairy cows in France allowed to graze periodically on the grass at the Palace of Versailles. These cows trace their lineage to beasts that once belonged to Charlemagne.

Maybe you still wouldn't drop $100 on a scoop of that strawberry ice cream, but I bet you'd spend a minute thinking about it. You'd pause to reflect on how much you really do love strawberry ice cream and how a dollar scoop of chocolate seems pretty chintzy. You'd spend a minute running down the list of things for which you'd been saving that $100. You might even ask yourself what money is good for if not to let loose every once in a while and treat yourself to something spectacular. Heck, maybe $100 is a steal for ice cream of such rarified genealogy. And, if I saw the look of hesitation in your eye and started offering to discount the price, to bring that $100 scoop down to $90, then to $75, then to $50—at some point you might change your mind. At some point you would sit up and say, "Okay, what the hell, I'll take it," and you will reach into your pocket to dig out that $50 or $30 or $10 or $5.50, whatever price point tipped you from the "No way" column to the "All right, let's do this" column. It's the point at which the utility you assign to your preference for strawberry ice cream aligns with your willingness to meet the price at which it is being offered. At that point, whether you realize it or not, you have become an economist, and a good one at that. You didn't even need to waste five years getting a PhD.

If you really want to earn your wings, consider what would happen after I sold you that $100 scoop. After you'd tried it, savoring those juicy French heritage strawberries and delighting in every swallow of that highly pedigreed ice cream, how much value would you place on a second scoop? I'm guessing it'd be hard to talk you into plunking down big bucks for another round. This is what economists like to call the law of diminishing marginal utility. The value you place on each next, or marginal, scoop declines steadily to the point that you may not want any more of that life-changing ice cream even if I offered it to you for free. Not many people will ever find themselves in such a sad situation, however, because we live in an environment of scarcity and I made up all that stuff about the Champagne strawberries and Charlemagne's cows. Even if I hadn't, and even if you had an essentially unlimited ice cream budget, everything we know about human nature tells us that you'd decide one day that you'd had enough.

Margin Call

One of the things economists like to say is that a rational person seeks to "maximize" his utility in most situations. Break it down. We've already defined utility, but what is a rational person? That's another term that gets thrown around an awful lot in economics. Most would say it's someone who makes calculated decisions based on a clear-eyed assessment of facts and evidence rather than emotion or impulse. That's fine, but an economist would say it's someone who makes decisions that increase rather than reduce utility. In everyday parlance, "to maximize" might as well mean "to get as much as you can." This may be how the germ of the idea that free market economists think greed is good was planted in some impressionable young minds. But maximizing doesn't mean that you seek to be happy all the time or that there are no limits to the amount of strawberry ice cream someone can consume. Of course there are limits. There are always limits! Remember that utility is synonymous not with usefulness but satisfaction. That's about striking the right balance, not taking more than you need. You can have too much of a good thing. Why? Because life is about trade-offs, even with things that give you great utility. The maximal outcome is one that keeps competing (and complementary) interests in balance.

Use your imagination for a second. It's a Saturday night at the start of summer. You're at the county fair with your friends, strolling down the fairway taking in all the attractions—the fortune teller, the go-karts, the bumper cars. There's so much to do, but since you only brought $20 you know you are going to have to make some choices. You live in an environment of scarcity, after all, and you are mindful that you have to give up something of value to get something of value, so you know intuitively that your double sawbuck is only going to go so far. You're even aware of the opportunity costs involved in spending your precious Saturday evening here at the fair and not somewhere else. You could be at the movies with your friends. Or you could be working an overtime shift, putting some new money in your pocket instead of looking for ways to spend the money you already earned.

The county fair is about more than just rides and attractions. It's about food too. You haven't eaten all day and your stomach is growling. There's no $100 French strawberry ice cream but there's plenty to choose from: deep-fried stuff, caramel apples, oversize pretzels, corndogs, square pizza on paper plates. They've even got blooming onions. The whole thing is a red-white-and-blue bacchanalia of gigantism and excess, and you are absolutely chomping at the bit to stick your face into the feedbag. You worked all week for this. The aroma from the popcorn machine moves up your nose like a fishhook, reeling you slowly, steadily in. You came here to maximize your Saturday night and live that salty, buttery, partially hydrogenated American dream.

Then something catches your eye—something you loved as a kid but haven't had in ages: cotton candy. You move as if pulled by an electromagnet. Your right hand is digging in the pocket of your jeans as you flash a single finger to the teenager behind the machine. He unsheathes a cardboard cone, jams it into the twister, and with a subtle turn of wrist pulls up a bouquet of glistening pink attic insulation. What you're looking at is pure sugar that has been tinted with food coloring, heated, liquefied, spun through a colander, and rapidly cooled into a pillow of wispy strands. You know it's wrong but you don't care. You pay. You grip the cone. Your friends laugh at how big the cotton candy is compared to your head. Everyone is having a great time.

"You're all having some," you say, in a semi-threatening but totally fun and yet totally serious way.

They do have some, greedily pinching off portions for themselves. At first the cloud of cotton candy resists separation from itself, but then it relents, stringing out limply like fluorescent corn-husk hair. The first bite is delicious. Everybody smiles with their eyes as it melts in their mouths. The fun and laughter build toward the second bite, but the thrill peaks immediately. Maximization has been momentarily achieved. It hangs like a punted football in the air. At the third bite, the fun is over. Everyone is disgusted with themselves. You and your friends wish you could turn back the clock and skip the cotton candy altogether. The uneaten portion, which is most of it, goes straight into the trash, and everybody goes off in search of some water with which to wash off the Kool-Aid stains on their fiberglass tongues.

You have just had a hard, hard lesson in the concept of diminishing marginal utility. Each next bite of cotton candy yields less pleasure, less benefit, less satisfaction than the one before. Why does it matter? Because not all utility is positive. You can have negative utility just like you can have negative preferences and negative satisfaction. By the third mouthful of cotton candy you are experiencing a sensation that goes by many names—disdain, abhorrence, barfvergnügen—and which can be just as formative as your positive preferences. Our choices are driven nearly as often by what we don't like as they are by what we do. Sometimes we screw up. Our preference mechanism fails us, or fools us, and we make decisions we regret. If you're lucky enough to live in a place where the long, dumb arm of the nanny state doesn't reach, the free market allows you to make bad choices every once in a while. Isn't it good to be an American?

The third bite of cotton candy demonstrates something else important about how we make economic decisions. The reality is that most of them are made at what economists call "the margins." All that means is that things don't happen in a vacuum. You made the economic decision to lay out the money for the cotton candy. It was a rational decision because you expected to increase your utility, but that wasn't the end of the economizing. The decision to chuck the half-eaten cone in the bin was an economic decision too, and was equally rational. Your utility was in sharp decline and you had no expectation that another bite of Mr. Nasty McPinkpuffin would turn things around. When we consume strawberry ice cream or cotton candy, we are usually looking at the question of how much to have not in an absolute sense but in a relative one: how much *more* or how much *less*. What do I get from the first bite? What do I get from the last bite? How much utility does the next hour of work, the next month of early morning exercise, or the next year of expensive education offer? What are the costs of a little more or a little less investment in something? What are the benefits?

The important stuff in life happens at the margins. It's the borderline, the place of exploration, the place where equilibrium can be found and achieved. It's also the place where you can totally screw things up. Every tabletop game of Jenga hinges on the marginal piece—the next piece to get pulled from the pile. Only one piece will be the piece that brings the tower down. Your choice matters. In an environment of scarcity, the margins are where you define utility, both positive and negative, and experience satisfaction, however you define it. Life is lived at the margins.

CHAPTER 5

PRICES

Johnny Rotten, pale and spotty, crouched at the foot of the abandoned drum riser, exhausted after 57 minutes of yowling. He looked disgusted, both with the 5,000 or so aging hippies in the audience at San Francisco's Winterland Ballroom and at the way the yowling had gone. With a contemptuous laugh befitting his status as punk rock's leading loudmouth, Rotten barked one of the great rock 'n' roll questions: "Ever get the feeling you've been cheated?"

His question—and his contempt—lingered in the air like the stink of stale sweat as the microphone thudded on the floor and the band left the stage. It was January 1978. The Sex Pistols, for whom Rotten was lead singer and chief provocateur, had just bashed out the final chord of their last rollicking, bollocking live show (at least until a reunion brought the surviving members back together two decades later). The pioneering punks had taken the British music world by storm the previous year, but the band was now finished after one album and a single underwhelming US tour. Rotten was only 22. Sid Vicious, the band's slender, pogoing "bassist," was 20. He didn't know it, but he had only a year left to live.

The Sex Pistols' meteoric slash through pop culture crashed to earth for what look like inevitable reasons now: They were young, experimenting with all sorts of drugs, and appeared to have low personal opinions of each other. It is according to this formula that all bands break up. No mystery there. There's always a price to pay. The mystery, at least for me, is the question. "Ever get the feeling you've been cheated?"

What an epic way for a rock band to go out. On its face, the question asks not for an answer but for agreement. It's a bit like saying, "Do you breathe air?" Yeah, sure, we all do. Everyone's had the feeling of being cheated. Maybe you paid full price for a newly released book only to see it on sale for 50% off at another bookstore just down the street. That could make you feel like a real dupe. Maybe you've had the experience of ordering takeout from a restaurant and, upon opening the bag to find a single packet of ketchup and no napkins, wondering whether the people who run the place would dare to serve such a measly portion of french fries to a sit-down customer. That's what it feels like to be played for a fool. I once paid cash money to a scalper outside Yankee Stadium for what turned out to be a forged ticket for a late-season, weeknight game against the Baltimore Orioles. The deal seemed too good to be true and it was. I only found out when the stadium ticket-taker laughed in my face as I tried to pass through the turnstile. Of course the scalper was long gone by that time. He ripped me off properly.

Then there is the feeling of being cheated not by how people in the world around you act when they try to get one over on you but by the way the world actually is—how it works, not in some fantasy version of how the world should work but in the real version of brick and mortar, flesh and blood, here and now. That's a bigger feeling, a background feeling, and a lot of people have it. They look at life, society, the world around them, and they just don't understand why things have to be the way they are. They think the rules should be different and don't like not being able to change them. They look at how we live and feel deeply unsatisfied. They look at the free market economic forces that reward people they consider unworthy and punish the righteous—and aren't we all a little bit righteous sometimes?—and they feel cheated.

A Sweet Science

Economics is sometimes called the "dismal science" by those who find themselves exhausted by economists' gloomy forecasts. Everybody dreams of a free lunch. Everybody wants something for nothing. Economists remind us that we'll have to pay eventually, because resources are scarce and life is about trade-offs. The dismal science tag also sticks to economics because of economists' frequent failures to predict the future with anything resembling accuracy. I guess someone somewhere decided that economics was one big cheat, so it became the dismal science. But it's a slur. Economics is not dismal. It is the sparkling art of decision-making. It's a brilliant and brightening way of looking at how and why people do the things they do. Adam Smith was a philosopher, and throughout most of history economics was rightly understood as a subset of that discipline. Many of the sharpest economists deserve to be called philosophers for the insights they provided into how we do live, could live, and should live. Economics relies on logic and in many cases assumes that people behave rationally. It also involves ethics and investigates abstract concepts like utility and dissatisfaction.

I've often suspected that the "dismal science" label was really an expression of lament about the unavoidable human realities on which economics shines a harsh light: As the Rolling Stones said, you can't always get what you want. Since we are humans, with appetites and desires, tastes and preferences, we tend to want things that we can't have, and most of the time we don't just want one or two of those things. Because we seek to maximize our utility, we want things that we can't have in larger quantities than could be considered necessary. If one is good, two is probably better, and we might as well get three just to be on the safe side. But while we can't always get what we want, sometimes when we look around we see people who are no better or smarter or harder-working than us but who seem to have plenty of what we want. We can't figure out why they get to have so much of what we want while we have so little, or maybe even none. It doesn't seem fair. We spend a lot of time stewing about it. Life can be so disappointing. We sometimes feel cheated.

What is it that keeps us from getting the things that we desire to have? What's the big obstacle standing in the way of our satisfaction? A religious person might suggest that our sinful nature is the reason. A psychoanalyst might propose that we don't get nice things because we don't think we deserve them. The answer I'm looking for is a little less lofty. Generally we don't get the things we want because we can't afford them. Our available resources don't align with our desires in a given moment. I have a computer, but it would make my life easier to have a better one. I have a car, but I wouldn't mind a safer and more comfortable one. I have a house, but I'd like a bigger one, maybe in a better location, perhaps with a private beach. And my family and I are lucky enough to get away for a vacation once or twice a year, but I can think of a few slightly more exotic travel destinations than the mundane locales we frequent that I'd like to cross off my list.

So what's preventing me from upgrading my current circumstances? Why do I drive a minivan instead of a sports car, and why do I vacation at my mother-in-law's house rather than at a private resort? There are a few reasons. I genuinely prefer driving a minivan over a sports car. But the main reason I can't live a life full of the luxuries I desire is that I can't afford them. Or, to be a little more socially scientific about it, I've taken stock of my preferences, made a mental accounting of my available resources, calculated the trade-offs in terms of the opportunity costs, and made peace with the fact that life is not determined by what I want but rather by the choices I make, so I had better make good choices about the investment and expenditure of my limited cash balance and credit.

To make good choices we need good information. In a market system the best piece of information available to anyone trying to make an economic decision is price. How much is the thing that I want going to set me back? What's the damage? Naturally I want to take a lengthy vacation on a sun-drenched Caribbean island. But I can't make an informed decision about whether to drop the dough until you tell me how much it's going to cost.

The Price Is Always Right

My son is into Lego, the Danish-made interlocking brick toys that you had better not call "Legos." He's shifting into the teenage gear now, but since about the age of five he's found a great deal of satisfaction from taking a few hours out and disappearing into the basement to assemble, disassemble, and reassemble his Lego sets. He has a small (too small, if you ask him) workspace dedicated to his preferred diversion. He emerges only when he's finished constructing a mini-replica of the Taj Mahal or the *Star Wars* Nebulon-B Frigate 77904. The kid has a lot of homework and school stuff to worry about, but doing Lego mellows him out. He's a young guy, but he understands that his pastime helps him decompress, and he loves it.

What he doesn't understand, or has yet to figure out, is why it's so expensive. Lego sets are costly. For the most part they are dearer than the average toy. As I write, the aforementioned Nebulon-B Frigate, from the *Star Wars Mandalorian*-themed collection, is retailing for north of $120. Only princelings and trustafarians can afford to buy toys at those prices. Your average American teenage ganglion can't see the logic of a price that seems so inflated for building blocks made of extruded plastic. It weighs on my guy. He asks me all the time, "Why do Lego sets have to cost so much?" He feels cheated.

Of course I feel bad for the boy. One of the hardest things for a young mind to understand is that a price is not an arbitrary thing. The makers of a product like Lego don't simply slap any old number that pops into their heads onto the tag on the package and jam it onto the shelves. Most of the time people won't buy a thing that is priced too high, and often they'll buy too much of a thing that is priced too low. But what is too high? What is too low? The trick for someone who is selling a product is, like Goldilocks, to get the price just right. You can do it by trial and error—set a price that you think is fair and adjust based on what happens—but most sellers opt for a slightly more rigorous approach, taking into account their accumulated costs and expectations of profit. However Lego goes about setting prices for their toy sets, they sure don't pull them out of their floppy Danish hats.

A price is the single most important data point in any market. It tells suppliers how much to produce and consumers how much to buy. It's a visible, tangible expression of forces that are otherwise invisible and intangible, namely supply and demand. The mysterious equilibrium reached by the aggregation of all the supply and all the demand for a particular good or service crystallizes into what is called the market-clearing price. If left alone to work as intended, the market will move toward this price even if it isn't set quite right to begin with. A high price tells the people who make that thing or provide that service that they should supply more of it, that the world is dying to get its hands on what they're selling. As that demand is satisfied, the price comes down. A low price tells those makers and sellers to pull back; there's too much of their stuff out there, and people don't need or want any more of it at the moment. As demand dries up, the price starts to rise until it reaches that perfect equilibrium.

The essayist Henry Hazlitt called demand and supply "two sides of the same coin." They exist in concert and actually reflect the same market impulses in negative image. "Supply creates demand because at bottom it *is* demand," wrote Hazlitt. "The supply of the thing they make is all that people have, in fact, to offer in exchange for the things they want." The supply of Lego constitutes the demand of all the people at Lego Group's Denmark headquarters for cars, bikes, food, and other goods. Demand begets supply; supply begets demand; the price is the sweet spot where the magic of exchange happens.

A price is like a musical note; it rings true. When a singer sings on pitch, she tries to hit the center of the note. She wants the sound she makes to resonate at the proper frequency. She doesn't want to be sharp or flat; she doesn't want to sing the wrong note. When she misses the center of the note, whether she means to or not, the sound itself betrays the mistake. It interacts poorly with the accompaniment. It creates disharmony and distortion, offending the ear. A wrong price is still a price, just like a wrong note is still a note, but it throws everything out of whack. A bad price corrupts a market transaction the same way a bum note ruins a concert.

Prices coordinate markets. Like buoys on a lake, they help market participants—buyers and sellers—navigate when they can't see shore. They provide markers on an unmapped route. Where else can a company like Lego get actionable information about what toys to produce and in what quantity? Lego doesn't have unlimited resources (nobody does), so it can't simply make and bring as many toy sets to market as it *thinks* its customers will want to buy. And it also can't afford to lose money when it sells them. It needs to organize itself to be profitable or else—and this is important—what's the point? The people who own and run Lego don't make toys only because they enjoy it. If I had to guess I'd say they probably actually do enjoy making toys, but like you, me, and the rest of the world, they can't afford to make toys simply because my son or your son or anybody's son gets great utility out of playing with Lego when their homework is done. The Danes who run Lego don't even know my son; how could that be their motivation?

No, they make and sell plastic toys to make a profit so they can pay themselves, grow and sustain the business, and take care of themselves and their families. That's it. And to make a profit they need to get more money from selling their toys than they spend to make them. If they succeed, they will have made my son, your son, and everyone else who loves Lego very happy, but—and this is also important—that can never be more than a secondary concern or they will find themselves bankrupt and out of business before too long. Then no one gets any Lego, and the sum total of human happiness is depleted. Then people will really feel cheated. We don't want that.

Think about it. Lego has to plan ahead. It has to order the stuff it uses to make the plastic that it uses to make the toys. It has to hire engineers and manufacturers and to manage all sorts of business processes like brand development, licensing, and product tie-ins before getting the product into packaging and onto trucks, trains, and ships bound for the places where its toys are sold. It has to advertise. There's a lot it must do before my son can walk into a store like Walmart or the local pharmacy and buy a 1,368-piece *Lord of the Rings* Battle of Helm's Deep Lego set. They can't simply wing it. What information other than price do they have with which to make decisions about which toys to make and bring to market? They could ask their customers, but how would they find them? I suppose they could perform a survey and ask everyone in the world what they want and how much they'd be willing to pay for it. That would be quite costly and surely pretty inefficient.

The wholesalers and retailers who actually interact with customers like my son have a better idea of how much demand there is for the stuff that goes on their shelves— because they see the results. If a toy sits there day after day and nobody buys it, the price is probably too high; at a lower price shoppers might go for it. If a toy sells out right away, the price is probably too low. They're missing out;

they could be getting more for that toy. The price mechanism—transmitted up through a complex web of middlemen like toy stores, retailers, and wholesalers—gives the corporate big shots at Lego the information they need about how much they should produce. On their own they'd never be able to pinpoint the right price with anything like the accuracy of the customer-facing toy store.

What about the other side of the transaction? What about my son, standing there in the aisle of the toy store, doing the mental math, trying to figure out whether it's worth it for him to drop his allowance on that Lego set or save it for something else. The price tells him what he needs to know as well. It gives him some concrete information to work with as he weighs his trade-offs and considers how much he really wants to buy those bricks. A high price represents giving up more of something that he values (his allowance, which is derived from the work he does around the house); a low price would enable him to have more of another thing he values (Lego). Whether the utility gains are worth the trade-offs are entirely up to him, but at least he has some data to work with and doesn't have to wing it.

The price, and the toy-buying public's reaction to it, also helps Lego know when it's time to switch things up a little in the product department. Any business that wants to survive in a market economy needs to develop new and better offerings, to innovate. Lego needs to throw a steady stream of appealing new toy sets at kids like my son or else—and this, too, is important—what's the point? Nobody needs Lego. It's a toy. Anyone could live without it. Even my son could live a satisfied and fruitful life with no Lego in it, though he wouldn't necessarily agree. What keeps him coming back is the enjoyment—the, ahem, utility—he gets from unboxing and building new designs that thrill and excite him. He has to find a Lego toy worth his time and money or he'll spend those precious (and scarce) resources elsewhere.

In the free market, Lego needs to innovate or it will die. Someone will come along with a better, cheaper, cooler option and eat Lego's proverbial lunch. That it hasn't happened so far is a testament to Lego's success in the dog-eat-dog environment of the international toy game. In a command-and-control economy, toy makers don't need to figure out the right price or find ways to satisfy customers. They don't need to innovate or turn a profit. In a socialist system, the sole incentive any business has is to keep the powers that be satisfied. If the toys stink and the kids are sad, well, who cares? So long as the central planners are happy we can keep on trucking.

If You Have to Ask

Back to my son's question: Why do Lego have to be so expensive? The answer—which he won't like, and you may not either—is that they actually aren't expensive. "Expensive" is like "hot" or "spicy": a relative concept, open to interpretation, dependent on context. The toys my son desires are expensive *to him* and to anyone who, like him, is in the position of either not having the money to pay for what he wants or having the money and not wanting to part with it. But "expensive" isn't an objective value. A stranger who asked you how much something cost wouldn't necessarily be able to understand what you meant if you replied, "It's expensive." As the old saying goes, if you have to ask, you probably can't afford it.

My son thinks Lego are expensive because the market sets their price at a level above that which he's personally willing to pay. Someone (Dad) will probably pay that price, but if no one does, the price will eventually come down. Supply meets demand and demand meets supply at an equilibrium, and that's the price of the Lego. You either consider it expensive or you don't. What my son thinks is an outrageous price could be one that I find entirely reasonable. We have different resource allocations and different sets of preferences, which aren't always aligned. We are confronted by different opportunity costs, and our choices are limited by our individual consideration of different sets of trade-offs.

"But it's not fair," I can just hear my son arguing. "You can afford it and you don't even want it, while I want it and I can't afford it." Maybe it is unfair. Maybe it isn't. Maybe it just is what it is. Who said life was going to be fair?

You know Pig-Pen, that *Peanuts* character who plays for Charlie Brown's baseball team although he never seems to have taken a bath? Questions and complaints about fairness follow discussions of economics like the cloud of dust that follows Pig-Pen. You can never get away from them. And, like the word "expensive," what's fair and unfair is entirely subjective. What should a price be? How much should a company like Lego supply of a particular toy set? Economists like to call these *normative* questions. Their answers vary according to the opinions and preferences of the people to whom the question is posed. If you ask my son, he'd say Lego should be free. If you ask Lego, they'd say they'd like to charge a lot more than they do. What the price is and what it should be are not just two different questions; they're two different types of questions. One has a real answer; the other is up to you.

Life Is Not a Box of Lego

Perhaps you are saying to yourself: This discussion is all fine and good for toys. People can live without Lego, but there are some things that people can't live without. What about food and water? How can prices for those essential things be left up to a profit-seeking market when lives could potentially be at stake if the people or companies who supply them decide that they can't make a buck doing so? Some may take the question further by defining access to a whole host of stuff as not just important or essential but as human rights—things that can't and shouldn't be left to the whims of the market. These include, in no particular order, clothing, electricity, legal representation, health care, housing, birth control, and even a basic income. In this view, the prices of these important goods and services should be controlled by an external force other than supply and demand.

"Because economics is a study of cause and effect, it deals with incentives and their consequences," writes Thomas Sowell in his 2000 book *Basic Economics*. "It has nothing to say about the validity of social, moral, or political goals such as 'affordable housing,' a 'living wage' or 'social justice.'" His point is simple: You may wish that the price mechanism had no influence on the supply of goods and services you deem essential, but it does. It always has and it always will. There's no such thing as "free" when it comes to the allocation of resources, even those things that are necessary for life. Interrupting the work done by the price mechanism ensures, in fact, that resources will be *misallocated*. Those that don't really need water, clothing, electricity, legal representation, health care, housing, and income will consume (at the margins) more than they would if those things were priced accurately. The people that really, truly need those things will find them difficult to come by because the price mechanism has been disengaged. More often than not those goods will be supplied, but in the absence of the price mechanism to determine who gets them and in what quantity, they won't be allocated fairly or efficiently.

Because people will buy more of a thing when prices are low and less of a thing when prices are high, controlling prices frequently has an effect on how much of that thing people will want to buy, or what economists call quantity demanded. The same causal relationship works in reverse for quantity supplied: the lower the price, the less supplied; the higher the price, the more supplied. So any form of a price control that keeps supply and demand from meeting at the magical, market-clearing price will distort a market—even one for things people can't live without—by giving consumers and producers the wrong signals about how much to consume and how much to produce. There are some who would like to interfere with the price mechanism by banishing it entirely, as if such a thing were possible. Prices exist even when you don't know what they are. As Pablo Escobar said, in a somewhat derivative context, "Everyone has a price. The important thing is to find out what it is."

Those who promise "free" college, "free" health care, and all manner of other "free" goods often have to work hard to obscure the obvious caveats, the most important of which is that someone will pay, just usually not the person on the receiving end of the allegedly free things. Free lunches, as nice as they sound, aren't really "free," not in the sense that butterflies are free. Someone always pays. But a more important reality to bear in mind is that price is only one way of rationing scarce goods. There are other ways. In societies that purport to offer "free" health care, people often have to wait for absurdly long periods of time for doctor's appointments and "nonessential" procedures. You can call it free if you like, but you pay with money or you pay with time.

The Problem of Inflation

To make good choices you need good information. Prices, as I have been saying, make the economic world go round. They are the best information available in a market transaction, and a free market worthy of the name can't operate without them. They ensure fairness and they ensure efficiency, by which I mean nothing is wasted in the economic sense. The supplier relies on price to help determine how much to produce and the consumer relies on price to determine how much to buy. Without good prices, buyers and sellers would be lost at sea.

You've probably had the experience of shopping in a grocery store and coming across an item that has been accidentally mispriced. My teenage friend Carl Pisarek worked weekends and summers throughout high school as a stock boy at the local ShopRite. He'd roam the store with a price-tagging gun in a low-slung holster, printing out stamp-sized labels like a heavy metal quickdraw artist and affixing those little stickers to soup cans. It was an important job. It was also a manual-input scenario, and so subject to human error. He had to get it right. Then as now, people shop on price in the grocery store. If Carl was distracted trying to get the fingering of a Randy Rhoads guitar solo right in his head, he could easily misread a number, transpose a 5 for a 2, or label the wrong item. A few cents this way or that can make the difference for some shoppers. Nowadays the job is bar-coded, with prices generally advertised beneath the items on the shelf. You bring it up to the checkout and the price scans automatically into the computer. But sometimes the price is wrong. Either it doesn't match what you saw in the aisle or it strikes you as screwy for some other reason, and you have to risk the ire of the people behind you in line to ask the cashier to check the price. It's embarrassing to stand stoically waiting with your cart while everyone else in the store quietly fumes that you are wasting their time, but no one is going to pay $15 for a box of cookies that are supposed to be $5.

Whether it's a box of cookies or a car, when you suspect a good is mispriced—or know it for sure—it changes how you behave. Economics is about choices, and bad information makes for bad choices. Prices, to a great degree, dictate economic behavior, so for the economy to work as it is supposed to they have to be reliable. It's essential. Grocery store mistakes can be quickly and easily remedied, but there are forces at play in an economy that can send prices screwy on a wider scale. These are much harder to fix and ultimately much more dangerous.

Prices of most things go up over time. We're all familiar with the idea. Everyone has heard a story—from a grandfather, grandmother, or elderly neighbor—about how ice cream used to cost a nickel back in the day. Once, when I was about 10, two friends and I hatched a plot to go to McDonald's and get some burgers and fries. I told my friends that I had a brilliant idea. I would ask my dad for some money to go to McDonald's, but I'd ask for more than I needed and with the extra I would treat them. My friends thought it was a grand plan, as did I. The conversation with my dad went something like this:

"Dad, I'm going to go to McDonald's and get a burger and some fries. Can I have some money?"

"Sure, son. How much do you need?"

"Oh, I think $5 ought to cover it."

"Five dollars? That's ridiculous. You don't need that much money to go to McDonald's, do you? Here's $1.50. That oughta take care of you. Get yourself a shake, too."

This was sometime around 1984. I'd asked my dad for $5 to go to McDonald's and he instantly smelled a scam. Nearly 40 years later I could still buy a McDonald's cheeseburger with that $1.50 from 1984, but not much else. A meal I could have had for somewhere between 50¢ and 70¢ back then goes now for just about the $5 I dinged my old man for (shake included).

Prices for things like cheeseburgers and french fries go up over time for lots of reasons, most of them pretty mundane. So long as it happens slowly and predictably, most people can incorporate this slow-motion inflation into their lives without too much trouble. Your income—which, if you work for wages or a salary, is the price of your labor—also increases over time, hopefully, so you pay more for the things you need but you have more to pay for them. When movements in price fall in line with people's overall expectations, they can plan for and absorb those changes without too much pain. It's when they can't plan for price changes, or when changes in their own incomes don't align with a general rise in prices, that things can get choppy.

Broad and systemic inflation is a pernicious economic disease with complicated causes of the sort I promised you in the introduction not to talk too much about. These range from the monetary policy pursued by central bankers and the levels of taxing and spending that the government does. Running an inflationary policy can be seductive for political leaders who have borrowed a lot of money to pay for things they want to do. Inflation punishes savers by diminishing the value of what they've stashed away, but it rewards borrowers since the money they will use to pay back their loans is worth less than the money they borrowed. Most people are both savers and borrowers, so the effect is a bit of a wash. But the government is mostly a borrower and not a saver, so politicians sometimes play inflationary games in hopes of erasing the debts they've run up trying to buy favor with the people. They had better know what they're doing, though, because voters can be unforgiving with regard to pocketbook issues.

Socially, politically, economically, mentally—inflation's effects are wide-ranging, corrosive, and erosive. Inflation causes governments to collapse and societies to crumble. It makes people crazy as they watch the money they've stashed in the bank slowly lose its purchasing power. Perversely, the smart thing to do during an inflation is to pull your savings out and buy things you don't necessarily want or need lest the price goes up—again. This is not good for the overall economy, as producers get confusing and often indecipherable signals about how much to supply.

The expectation of inflation can be just as deadly to the smooth functioning of an economy as the real thing. It distorts investment decisions and causes capital to be misallocated. Everyone in the economy starts looking for a safe harbor and the effect is compounding. It's like speeding in a car and hitting a patch of ice. Whipping the wheel around in a frenzy to try to gain some purchase on the asphalt only makes you spin out more wildly. The historical examples of the damage inflation can do are numerous and recent. You may have seen photos on the internet of the $100 trillion bill from Zimbabwe, an economic basket case ruled into the ground over 50 years by the autocrat Robert Mugabe, the last man in the world to rock a Hitler mustache. In Weimar Germany, laid low by the Allied surrender terms after World War I, workers would show up with wheelbarrows to collect their wages on payday. Inflation was so potent that the money would be practically worthless in a few days. The joke was that if you got robbed on the way home the thief was probably after your wheelbarrow.

Honestly, inflation is no joke. It's like a venomous snake coiled up in a basket. Policy makers are smart to leave the basket alone. Sometimes it's unavoidable. During wartime, borrowing and printing money can be a matter of national survival. If the government doesn't spend, spend, spend to win the war, there may not be a country left to pay back its debts. This money floods the economy and causes inflation. So be it. Let the snake out of the basket on the full understanding that when the crisis passes you'll have to figure out a safe way to get him back in again. Every once in a while, however, a politician or a central banker comes along and makes a big show out of kicking the basket while saying, "I ain't afraid of no stupid snake." God have mercy on the people who live in that country.

From my point of view, keeping inflation under control is an entirely laudable approach to economic policy. It's no mystery to me why policy makers would want to keep that snake in the basket. Most economists would agree, however, that a little inflation is necessary to "grease the wheels" of an economy, to keep the whole unwieldy train moving forward. Responsible central bankers therefore set an inflation target and fiddle with the tools and policy levers at their disposal to try to get as close to the target as they can over time. If you've ever taught an overly cautious teenager how to drive, you know how dangerous and disorienting it can be to go too slow on the highway. But speed kills, so we have limits on our roads—targets, if you like. When you get it just right, when everyone on the road is in the neighborhood of the posted speed limit, traffic should flow nicely and everyone gets where they need to go safely. There are places in the economy, however, where the highway patrol has gotten a little overzealous. Out of a desire to achieve certain social outcomes, they have decreed that prices must not be allowed to rise in certain markets and that prices may not be allowed to fall in others. These price interventions can be just as discombobulating as general inflation and just as dangerous as a slow-footed teenager in the passing lane.

Control Patrol

If you grew up in the New York area in the 1970s and '80s, as I did, you will remember Crazy Eddie, the electronics store chain. Nobody I knew ever bought anything from Crazy Eddie, but everyone I knew was familiar with the commercials. They were a staple on afternoon television, which, now that I think about it, didn't make much sense. Teens and tweens flipping around looking for a melodramatic after-school special to watch don't typically have a budget for answering machines and stereo equipment. Anyway, the commercials were a hoot. They featured an antic middle-aged pitchman in a dark blazer over a light-colored turtleneck waving his hands like a lunatic and rattling off the store's featured deals. At Christmas time he'd be throwing around fake snow and shouting like a legitimate street-corner maniac: "It's Crazy Eddie's greatest stereo sale ever!" He spoke in triple-time, fast-forward, advertising patois before that style really took hold on the airwaves: "Wearenotundersoldwecannotbeundersoldandwewon'tbeundersold" . . . barely coming up for air before declaring with a finger to your face, "And we mean it!"

The guy in the commercials wasn't Crazy Eddie himself, as we would all learn later when the real Crazy Eddie went to federal prison for securities fraud, but the pitchman actor seemed kooky enough on the small screen that everybody assumed he was in fact Crazy Eddie. He became a local celebrity, up there with radio's Cousin Brucie and TV weatherman Lloyd Lindsay Young. No kid in New York, New Jersey, or Connecticut was unfamiliar with the Crazy Eddie schtick. Many aspiring young sidewalk showmen of my immediate acquaintance could perform the 30-second commercials in their entirety, with hand gestures and vocal cadence aligned in the service of perfect mimicry. Observers would all be waiting for the showstopping last line, delivered in a hurricane of Brooklyn brio, hands thrust forward and arms spread widely akimbo: "Crazy Eddie, his prices are *in-sane!*"

There have always been, and probably will always be, American political hucksters who, like Crazy Eddie, promise the world at prices that are *in-sane*. They boast of the ability to short-circuit the price mechanism to deliver good things to the public at no cost—at least no cost that you'll have to pay. Recent years have produced a bumper crop of Crazy Eddies promising all manner of utopian solutions to society's most complex problems. Free health care and free college are just the beginning. There's also free childcare and pre-K. Don't forget free broadband and free government cell phones. There's even free money in the form of a universal basic income. The prices for these valuable things aren't just "in-sane," they don't exist. There are no prices. Don't tell Pablo Escobar.

These politicians promising this bonanza of free stuff get the headlines, and their proposals consume a lot of the political oxygen, but the heat they generate often obscures the damage done by more pedestrian policies that interfere daily with the smooth functioning of the price mechanism. We call them price controls. They take two forms: price ceilings, which keep prices artificially low, and price floors, which keep prices artificially high. Both can be extremely destructive. Messing with the price mechanism is always a bad idea, even or especially if your intentions are good. The unintended consequences that result almost always make the problem you're trying to solve worse.

The classic example of the price ceiling is rent control. Sounds like a great thing. Nobody likes to pay rent. But when landlords are prohibited from charging the market-clearing price for housing, they supply less of it. Why? Because at the margins, where all economic decisions are made, it no longer makes sense for them to rent an apartment or house to a tenant. The extra income they receive from doing so isn't worth the added cost of maintaining a rental property and catering to tenants' needs. "But housing is a human right," you say. That's a fine sentiment, but apartments and rental homes don't grow on trees. They also don't heat themselves, paint themselves, or fix themselves when the pipes start leaking. Owners and landlords do those things. Contrary to popular belief, landlords do more than simply collect the checks once a month.

Rent controls also reduce turnover in rental markets, which means that renters will have difficulty finding apartments that suit their needs. Older people hang on to cheap apartments that may be larger than what they actually need because rent control has made it uneconomical for them to move out. While that may not seem like a problem on the face of it, you'd have a different view if you were the young parents of a growing family and had been on a waiting list for a larger apartment for months or even years. Rent control creates an incentive structure that makes it impossible for the market to work its magic by matching housing supply to rental demand. Paradoxically, a policy intended to make it easier for people to afford housing actually makes it harder for them to find housing in the first place.

Similarly distorted incentives present themselves in the labor market when a minimum wage is introduced. Wages and salaries are the price of labor. When an employer must pay a higher price than the market-clearing wage or risk breaking the law, he will reduce supply of the very thing that low-skilled employees are in the labor market to find—low-wage jobs. You may view this is a victory for human rights. I can assure you it is a defeat for the 16-year-old who is looking to take his first tentative step into the labor market. That kid, who is perhaps not college material and has no intention of working at the entry-level wage his entire life, has yet to find out what it feels like to cash an honest paycheck. Because the minimum wage has lopped off the lowest rung of the job ladder, he will spend his summer months or his after-school hours doing things that polite society might not put such a high value on. If we could find that kid and pose Johnny Rotten's question to him, I guarantee he'd have an answer.

CHAPTER 6

SPECIALIZATION

Take a look around the house. Have a peek in the basement, the medicine cabinet, your closet, or the freezer. I'll bet you'll find a lot of stuff, probably more than you need, maybe even more than you want. Dress shoes. Key chains. Laptops. Picture frames. Desks. Forks. Throw rugs. Coffee table books. Over-the-counter heartburn medication. Pens. Prescription blood-pressure pills. Vacuum cleaners. Frozen peas. A backscratcher. A shoehorn. A beer stein that says "Superdad." It's easy to take it all for granted. Ever wonder where it all comes from?

We live in an age of plenty, historically speaking, despite frequent dire pronouncements by politicians and television talking heads of imminent immiseration. Overstuffed attics, late-model cars, full refrigerators, and updated smartphones are a testament to the relative wealth of American civilization. If you take the time to think about how it all ended up in your house, you can't help but be amazed. Everything your eye beholds, from the lamp in your living room to the varnish on the slats of your wood floor, has traveled a long and often complicated road to be with you. The design process, the production decisions, the acquisition of raw materials, the fabrication, the safety inspections, the packaging, the shipping, the handling, logistics, marketing, shelving, selling—practically everything in your home has been on a months-long, if not a years-long, invisible journey, passed voluntarily from one set of skilled hands to another, shaped, stamped, cured, carved, extruded, painted, basted, boxed, binned, and bargain-basemented. Before it ever caught your eye at the retail store or in the online shop, that product had already lived quite an adventurous life. But where does it all come from? Who knows how to make all that stuff?

The answer is cool: nobody.

We, Pencils

Milton Friedman, the great free market explainer and evangelist, was fond of the pencil. It was his best prop.

Specialization

With appropriate credit to Leonard E. Read, author of the famous short essay "I, Pencil," Friedman used the thin yellow pencil on TV, in his lectures and writing, and even on the cover of his best-known book.

"Look at this lead pencil," Friedman implores the viewer in *Free to Choose*, his absolutely essential public television series. "There's not a single person in the world who could make this pencil. Remarkable statement? Not at all. The wood from which it's made, for all I know, comes from a tree that was cut down in the state of Washington. To cut down the tree it took a saw. To make the saw it took steel. To make the steel it took iron ore." You see where this is going?

No one person on earth knows how to make a pencil or could do it all on his own. The idea isn't that pencils aren't assembled in a pencil factory, or that they aren't sold by pencil sellers. They are. But even a product as apparently elementary as a yellow No. 2 pencil is actually a marvel, a miracle product made possible only by the free market forces of trade, supply, and demand—and one we haven't yet discussed: specialization.

So let's do it real quick, just to say we did: What is a pencil made of? I bet you think you know. First of all there's that West Coast American wood, grown by timber wizards over the course of who-knows-how-many years, logged, lumbered, and milled into relatively small blocks of wood. Some advanced machine, designed and refined by an imaginative engineer, takes pieces of that raw small lumber and turns them into pencil-shaped pieces. That's the kind of enviro-industrial commerce on which it seems likely that one person could have a pretty firm grasp. But then there's the lead, which isn't lead at all but graphite—aka plumbago—mixed with clay. The more clay the harder the "lead" in the pencil. In Friedman's day, graphite was mostly mined in Sri Lanka. Nowadays it comes from open-pit operations in Brazil and China, where it is often extracted through the unexpectedly mellifluous process called "beneficiation by flotation." I bet not even half the people who work in the graphite extraction industry could explain the process by which beneficiation by flotation is accomplished.

How does the graphite stick get inside the wood of the pencil? This is a question that lies somewhere in the mental space between brainteaser and cognitive short circuit. It could be the basis for an American Philosophical Association breakout panel. I promised you this wouldn't be a book for academics, so let's skip to the rubber eraser, called by pencilmen the "plug," which—surprise, surprise—isn't rubber at all but something called "factice." According to Friedman, factice is "a rubberlike product made by

Specialization

reacting rapeseed oil from the Dutch East Indies with sulfur chloride." The pink color of the eraser—er, plug—comes from cadmium sulfide, cooked up in a lab somewhere by a chemist who knows more than you do about inorganic compounds. A little piece of brass (known as the "ferrule") surrounds the plug to keep it from flying off as you rub it across the wrong answers on your math test. Brass is an alloy of copper and zinc. You only need a little of it to fabricate a pencil's ferrule, but copper and zinc mining are industries all to themselves, lousy with well-paid geologists, metallurgists, geophysicists, engineers, and monster-truck drivers. Do you think any of them know how to make a pencil? Seems like a long shot.

I hope you can see why Friedman loved pencils so much as a teaching tool. A pencil is such a seemingly simple everyday object, yet, when you stop and consider it, there's really no end to the complexity of how one is put together and brought to market. We didn't even touch on the yellow and black paint that gives the pencil its distinctive look. Wanna bet that even the one guy who can explain beneficiation by flotation is probably in the dark about how paint is made?

Now think of all the things in your house that you don't think of as simple everyday objects. Where to begin? You've got your washing machine, your dishwasher, your light switches, your smart speakers. You've got the car in your garage and the snowblower in your shed. You've got a machine that makes fresh cups of high-quality coffee with the touch of a button. Each one is a marvel of innovation and enterprise. When you sharpen and use a pencil, you are holding in your hand not a blunt instrument or a simple tool. It's the physical embodiment of an almost immeasurable amount of ingenuity, investment, and physical labor. Think about how much book learning and sweat equity goes into the creation of a smart TV. It's no day at the beach.

Topping it all off, as Friedman notes, is what the mere existence of the pencil, the compact car, and the smart TV says about voluntary cooperation in a free market: "None of the thousands of persons involved in producing the pencil performed his task because he wanted a pencil. . . . Each saw his work as a way to get goods and services he wanted—goods and services we produced in order to get the pencil we wanted. Every time we go to the store and buy a pencil, we are exchanging a little bit of our services for the infinitesimal amount of services that each of the thousands contributed toward producing the pencil." Friedman wanted to simplify things. He used the little lead pencil to illustrate the big idea: Markets are so good at figuring out what we need and giving it to us that it feels like some mastermind must be pulling the strings. But there is no mastermind; there's only the invisible forces of supply and demand coordinating market activity. The only thing you ever see is the pencil.

You Are My Special Angel

A pencil is a tangible thing, but consider what Friedman said about what we're doing when we go to the store to buy one. We exchange a portion of "our services" for a portion of "the services that each of the thousands contributed toward producing the pencil." Not all economic transactions involve things that get shipped in boxes or stocked on shelves.

The American economy doesn't make as many things as it once did. We are an advanced, post-industrial society. That means most of our considerable national wealth is generated by the provision of services, rather than the production of goods or the export of raw materials. That's not to say that everyone in America works in an office pushing papers around a desk or mousing numbers around a screen. But for the most part the US in the 21st century is a service-based economy. Sometimes we call it a knowledge economy. Much of what our most productive workers do is intangible. That wasn't so 100 or even 50 years ago. As recently as the 1950s the American economy was primarily built around manufacturing.

How did we get from there to here? It's been quite the journey, so let's go back a bit. The barter economy, based on a nomadic lifestyle of hunting and gathering, gave way to an agricultural economy about 12,000 years ago. Once people got the hang of growing their own, they began settling in one place for their entire lives and devoting their days to intensive cultivation of the land and domestication of certain useful livestock animals. They contributed their daily physical labor to the production of food and other raw materials that could then get laboriously turned into helpful things like rudimentary tools and basic clothing. It was difficult and time-consuming work, requiring hard labor from dawn to dusk, but as the generations passed, the knowledge accumulated. Farming techniques improved and yields grew larger. As people grew better at farming, they began producing more than they or their immediate family, friends, and relations could consume, leading to large surpluses that could be saved or traded. Some people had time for economically productive activities that took them out of the fields and into workshops, where they produced finished goods like advanced tools and functional—even fashionable—clothing. Others became bookkeepers or politicians. A few even became journalists.

Specialization

Societies eventually emerged that were denser and more complex than simple farming communities. Cities grew up around the most successful settlements. Whether you were a city, a city-state, a small country, or a big empire, your success or failure often depended on how thoughtfully you exploited and consumed your natural resources, how productive your workers were, and how well you managed your trading relationships. Not much has really changed.

One natural resource that has always been key to economic success is talent, a slippery thing, hard to put your finger on but also hard to ignore when you do. People, like nations, are blessed with different allocations of talent. Everybody gets dealt a different hand. Some of us are good with numbers, some of us have strong backs. Some of us can sing like birds, some of us can't carry a tune. It's easy and tempting to understand history's greatest social and scientific advances as the result of happy accidents—a handful of wheat dropped in just the right place at just the right time, a strange mold growing in an unattended petri dish in Sir Alexander Fleming's laboratory. But as often as not the greatest leaps forward were made by talented people working in jobs that suited them and through which they could make an oversize contribution to the sum of human happiness.

The age of agriculture lasted right up to Adam Smith's day. What brought it to an end and ushered in the Industrial Revolution is a matter of some debate. Technological change certainly played a big part. Developments in the fabrication of metals such as iron and steel, advanced understandings of the uses to which energy sources like coal and petroleum could be put, and new machines such as the steam engines and the spinning jenny all conspired to move people off the farm and into the factory, broadly speaking. But perhaps the most powerful factor wasn't a thing but an idea—the notion that individual workers could specialize in the production of a certain good, or a certain component in a manufacturing process, to the exclusion of others. By focusing on adding value in one particular aspect of a complex task rather than trying to master all or several aspects of that task, the worker in an industrial economy becomes more skilled. The highly skilled worker is marginally more efficient—he can do more in less time—which redounds to the benefit of the entire enterprise. When workers are more efficient they are more productive, and productivity, it turns out, is a key driver of economic success.

Specialization is like economic steroids. On the individual level it enables a worker to command higher wages because a more productive worker is more valuable to an employer than a less productive one. This is the reason people go to school to study a particular subject or acquire a particular skill. There are some jobs, of course, where it pays to be a jack of all trades—there's always a place on the team for a utility man—but in a service economy the really big bucks tend to flow toward those who can add value in large quantities by doing a rare thing extremely well. It helps explain why a guy who can hit a round ball with a round bat makes $30 million a year and a middle-school English teacher makes, well, less.

When it comes to a company, specialization improves the efficiency of the workers, which improves the efficiency of the overall operation by putting the available capital to the best use possible, allowing a company to improve its margins and compete more effectively for a larger share of the market. Think of an auto-parts supplier that makes just one piece of an engine and sells that to a big car manufacturer. Maybe the big car manufacturer once made all those parts itself but decided it couldn't do it all. Perhaps it realized the time had come to stop directing valuable capital, both human and financial, away from what it did best and let some other outfit that could perform those tasks more efficiently take the ball and run with it. Buying the parts from a company that specializes in making them—and only them—allows big car companies to focus on the things it does best, designing and assembling cars. This kind of thing happens all the time.

A very high percentage of new businesses started in the US are actually spinoffs from larger companies. If you make a habit of checking the obituaries published in the weekend edition of the *Wall Street Journal* you'll read some incredible life stories of highly successful people. Frequently the pivotal moment comes when the deceased realizes that the big company she's working for is missing out on a lucrative opportunity and, if she has the courage to strike out on her own, she can make the leap from being an ordinary employee to being her own boss. The greatest leaps forward are rarely the result of a lightning strike. More often they are derivative of an established business line and the result of specialization.

Press the Advantage

On the national level, specialization is how a country exploits its comparative advantage to trade with other countries in international markets for goods and services. The British economist David Ricardo first developed the idea of comparative advantage in the early 19th century. Ricardo, who was born into wealth, had an interesting life. He worked as a stockbroker, financier, and businessman.

Legend has it that he had somehow acquired inside information about the eventual outcome of the Battle of Waterloo in 1815 and bet big on Napoleon's defeat, netting himself a million pounds—a massive fortune at the time. A million pounds is still a lot of money on its own, but in today's money Ricardo's alleged haul was something like $100 million.

It's a good story, though probably not true. Ricardo had already made his mega millions well before the battle and had used it to retire, think, write, and buy himself a seat in the House of Commons. Proving that riches are no way of avoiding tragedy, he died at the relatively young age of 51. But he left behind a great contribution to classical economics. The theory of comparative advantage holds that countries can benefit from trade so long as each focuses on doing those things it can do most efficiently relative to other countries. The tally was to be measured in our old friend opportunity cost—the loss of potential gain from forgone options. A country should do what it does best while giving up the least, weighing the trade-offs just like people do.

Let's say it's David Ricardo's time, about 1818. There are two neighboring countries, Fleeceland and Burgessvilla, that are similar in size and have something like the same topography, weather, and population. One key difference between them is that Fleecelanders are really good at shearing sheep. They have an abundance of the beasty ruminants roaming their windswept pastures and dales, as well as a basically unlimited supply of experienced farmhands who simply love shearing sheep and are good at it. Fleeceland is in a great spot when it comes to wool. As a nation, it can shear sheep more efficiently (relative to other options) than just about anybody out there, including Burgessvilla, and it also has the ability to turn that raw wool into usable fabric more efficiently (relative to other options) than just about every other country, including Burgessvilla. Because of its new and exciting Industrial Revolution, Fleeceland is loaded to the gills with factories and workers that crank out bolts and bolts of finished wool cloth at a pace you wouldn't believe. Fleeceland doesn't do everything well, but it takes gold in both sheep shearing and wool finishing.

Nearby Burgessvilla feels overwhelmed by Fleeceland's success in the wool game. The Burgessvillians have sheep too, but they aren't quite as good as their show-off neighbors at shearing the wee buggers. They also aren't that great at taking their raw wool and turning it into finished fabric. They're okay at it, but not nearly as good as stupid Fleeceland, which is just annoyingly excellent at everything. Let's say, since it's 1818 in this little exercise, that the world is living through a historical moment in which wool and finished wool fabrics are extremely popular and highly sought after. They are the main things driving the global economy. Everybody loves wool, so lots of countries are trying to get into the wool game, Burgessvilla among them. But the Burgessvillians can't decide whether they should get into the raw wool side of things or the finished products side. They know they can't compete with Fleeceland, which does both things far better than they do. Perhaps if they put all their, uh, wool in one basket they could make a go of it. But which basket? Raw wool or finished products?

They need to do what David Ricardo said and weigh the opportunity costs. If Fleeceland is two or three times better at making finished clothes than Burgessvilla but five or even ten times better at sheep shearing, the theory of comparative advantage says that both countries will be better off if Fleeceland focuses on giving the sheep haircuts and leaves the clothes-making to Burgessvilla. The way to make the most of your comparative advantage is to specialize. Focus on doing the thing you do best while giving up the least. Recent history provides plenty of examples of poor or developing countries making use of their relatively cheap labor, a serious comparative advantage, to grow rich.

One caveat: For Fleeceland, betting it all on sheep shearing may make economic sense but it may be a national security mistake. What if Burgessvilla finally has enough of Fleeceland's general excellence and attacks, cutting off trade with the outside world? Fleeceland's leaders would probably be wise to keep a few textile factories in working condition even as they focus their national resources on supplying the world with their highly sought-after raw wool products. In the event of an emergency, they'll want to be able to fire those factories up again. Pretend we aren't talking about sheep and wool. There are survival-oriented industries like arms manufacturing or security-sensitive sectors like communications in which countries may wish to retain a certain competency. In the event of a showdown at the international O.K. Corral, you wouldn't want to be at the mercy of an enemy for something like bullets or phone batteries. Most countries will retain a little bit of this or that industry that it may not have a real comparative advantage in for the sake of ensuring the ability to ramp it up when the time comes, if the time comes.

Send Lawyers, Guns, and Butter

In a macro sense, countries have a lot of trade-offs to consider. All countries have limited amounts of wealth and face a version of the following choice: Spend those finite resources either on food for your people (which economists, being silly people, like to call "butter") or on protecting yourself (which economists, being suddenly very literal people, like to call "guns"). If you spend all your limited wealth on butter, there will be no money left over for guns, and vice versa. So the question becomes, how much of the one are you willing to give up so that you can obtain the other? In a perfect world we could have everything we want, but life isn't determined by what we want. It's determined by the choices we make. In an imaginary world, Fleeceland and Burgessvilla have to choose between sheep shearing and making wool clothing. In the real world, every country must choose between guns and butter, just like every person must choose between savings and consumption, work and leisure, and a limitless horizon of things we might like more of if we didn't live in an environment of scarcity.

The nation whose leaders have some inkling that they might soon be engaged in war will shift some of their scarce resources from the purchase or production of butter to the purchase or production of guns. By the same token, a nation that is at peace with its neighbors but worried about feeding a growing population of hungry citizens might trim the bazooka budget and invest a little more of its limited national wealth into ensuring that there is a chicken in every pot. Life, even for a great nation with a large and growing gross domestic product, is about trade-offs.

CHAPTER 7

WORK

I was raised, like many people, with the belief that some careers are fundamentally unselfish. These are the jobs that aren't really jobs but vocations, fueled by devotion and sacrifice and a commitment to participating in a cause that is greater than yourself. Let's call them social services or human services: teaching, healing, protecting, representing, educating, or advocating for those who can't do such things for themselves. Rarely are these jobs located within private business or industry. They are often public-sector jobs attached firmly or loosely, as the case may be, to a stream of government funding. There's even a special category for politicians, local and national, respectfully called "public service" (despite the uncanny private advantage that often accrues to those who pursue it). I was taught that these are the noble professions, the work people do not for a paycheck or a pension but to be of service. People pursue these careers because they care. They are driven by a strong desire to put something good into the world. Artists qualify, as do physical and psychological therapists and college professors, nurses and home health aides, social workers and nonprofit professionals. Librarians qualify. So do journalists, funnily enough.

Then there are careers that are fundamentally selfish. These are jobs that are not about serving others but are solely about serving yourself. These positions and career tracks are filled with people interested only in making as much money as they can. The primary things they care about are social status and net worth. Selfish-sector jobs include, in no particular order, finance, banking, accounting, advertising, consulting, all manner of for-profit concerns larger than a local landscaping business, most jobs that can't be easily explained to a five-year-old, some lawyers, and almost anything that happens in an office building or an industrial park.

Either you grow up planning to pursue a passion and fulfill a social purpose, or you grow up looking to fill your bank account. That's what I was raised to believe, and I hardly think I was the only one.

When I got older I recognized the folly—the peril, even—of making value judgments about people's career choices. For a start, many people don't have a choice. When it comes to putting bread on the table, you do what you have to. Suggesting otherwise betrays a bit of an elite bias. The children of the comfortable can afford to pick and choose. Pretty much everybody else takes whatever job pays the bills. They don't spend a lot of time worrying about the moral consequences of their decision to make a living.

But the main problem with valorizing particular lines of work is this: Who's to say that tax accountants and corporate vice presidents only do what they do for the money? Maybe they love their jobs. Maybe they enjoy them. I don't think I would derive any particular personal utility from, say, managing logistics for a global supply chain, but maybe those who do that kind of work genuinely think otherwise. Maybe it gives them a sense of satisfaction knowing that their daily efforts make it possible for parts and accessories to get where they need to go. Maybe they can see the bigger picture, and it makes them happy to know that they've played a small part in the production of goods that some people somewhere want or need enough to reach into their own pockets and pay for.

I'm not being a wise guy. I'm completely serious. A job that seems soul-destroying to you may give the person who does it a sense of dignity and purpose. How do you know? And why would you care? Somebody has to run logistics for a global supply chain. Perhaps it's the fulfillment of a lifelong dream. You just don't know. You can't know.

Moreover, who's to say that every teacher is a saint and every nurse is a hero? We know that isn't true. The papers are full of stories about people in these kinds of jobs who have abused the trust placed in them. And while everybody makes fun of lawyers for being particularly mercenary when it comes to the types of clients and behavior they are willing to defend, I have it on good authority that pretty much all of them think they are doing the Lord's work—and getting paid a little less than what they deserve to do it.

Thankful for the Work

"Daddy, why do you have to go to work? Why don't you just stay here with us?"

I have five kids, ranging in age from 18 to 5. Each of them has at some point looked me up and down as I'm heading out in the morning and asked me a version of that question. It's a rite of passage in our house.

"Well, I'd love to stay here with you, but if I don't go to work I won't get paid," is my stock answer. I've been at this a while, so I know what needs to come next. A five-year-old hasn't a clue what it means to get paid to do a job, so I have to go a little further and fill in the relevant details. "When I go to work they give me money. And I bring that money home and we use it to buy all this stuff like food and sneakers and the television. If I don't get paid for going to work, where are we going to get the money to buy cool toys to play with?"

This explanation is typically not robust enough to satisfy inquiring little minds. They might understand better if I told them that I got to play with my own cool toys all day, but then I'd have to explain that Daddy thinks words are toys and ideas are cool. Such an admission may do damage to my reputation around the house. I'm pretty sure at least one of my kids still thinks I work not at the world's best newspaper opinion page but at the train station where my wife drops me off every morning.

The fact is, I like my job. It challenges me and keeps me interested. The work is constantly new and exciting. No two days are totally alike. Showing up every day and getting the paper out gives me a great deal of satisfaction. Is it noble? Is it unselfish? Is it helping anyone? Actually, I think the *Journal* opinion pages help a lot of people, and I'm proud to contribute to them every day. Not everyone agrees that what we produce is a net benefit to society, however. So be it. That's the nature of the business. This is the life we chose.

My attachment to words and ideas aside, the main reason I stick with my job is that it provides me with the means to take care of my family. Like everyone, I've done plenty of jobs in my life that didn't give me either satisfaction or enough income to pay the bills. Many people get up every day and dread the thought of the 8 to 10 hours they'll have to spend at work. Most of us have our eye on something better. If a job comes along that pays more than our current position for the same (or less) work and, as an added bonus, offers the prospect of a greater challenge or more satisfaction, we'll usually jump ship. There are reasons why we might not, of course. Loyalty to colleagues or to a boss. Inertia—perhaps you are just the kind of person who hates change. Maybe you are embroiled in an office romance and nothing short of arrest could drag you away. Fine. Be grateful that you live in a society like ours—a diversified economy supporting many different types of industries and companies of all sizes that compete to find the most suitable workforce available at any given time. You have options. Not so everywhere in the world.

Fair Pay for Fair Play

Work, whatever form it takes, is an exchange. A worker trades his labor for wages, a salary, or even a one-time payment. That makes going to work an economic transaction, and economic transactions are what markets are made of. Labor has value and people don't simply give it away. Generally they rent it out. If you're an employer you must look for it, lure it, pay for it, and, most of the time, compete for it. Labor is a good like any other. Its price is determined by supply and demand. Some people are uncomfortable with the very idea of a market for labor, which is essentially a market for the time and energy of human beings, who only have one precious life to live. I guess a market for labor strikes some as being a little too similar to human bondage. I'm not sure how such people imagine decisions about who works where, for how long, and at what wages would be decided in a world without labor markets—which, by the way, are nonconcrete and weren't "invented" but rather emerged spontaneously. So long as people are fairly compensated for their time and energy, I don't see what the problem is. Disagreements about what constitutes fair compensation are a separate matter.

Usually we think of companies, factories, and businesses as the suppliers in a given market and consumers, workers, and families as the demanders. Honda sells minivans; I, the consumer with the five kids, buy them. In a labor market, it's the reverse. The workers control the supply side. They are the ones looking to sell. The employers control the demand side. They are looking to buy.

In well-functioning labor markets, with lots of employers offering the opportunity to work and lots of employees looking to take jobs, the price for labor reveals itself in the same way prices do in the markets for hamburgers, real estate, or Lego toys. If the worker doesn't consider the exchange fair, he doesn't enter into it. Same for the employer. That's not to say it can't get weird sometimes. People take jobs all the time that don't suit their talents or temperaments. Employers sometimes hire people not because they're right for the job and qualified to do it but because the work needs to get done and they're the only ones who answered the call. In a healthy labor market, with on-ramps and off-ramps galore, these mismatches are bound to be temporary.

"There is so much wealth in this country," my dear Aunt Sally would sometimes say. "If they can pay a ballplayer millions and millions of dollars a year, they can certainly afford to give teachers a raise."

I knew what she meant. There was a kernel of truth in what she said. A teacher has the ability to change a person's life for the better, to set them on a path to a happy and fulfilling life, and many good ones do just that. Hitting a round ball with a round bat successfully 3 times out of 10 doesn't, on its face, add much to society. So why is there such a huge gap between a teacher's take-home pay and a baseball slugger's annual haul? A lot of ballplayers who get stadium-size, guaranteed contracts aren't even that good. A guy hits .220 with nine home runs, sits out the second half of the year with "pain in the side," and still gets paid $10 million. A teacher gets up at the crack of dawn every morning to drive 45 minutes to the inner city, where he spends his day battling to make a difference in the life of even one kid, before coming home to a mailbox full of credit card bills. It doesn't seem right.

While I understood my dear Aunt Sally's frustration, I felt strongly, even as a child, that something was missing. A vital piece of the puzzle had been left out. A ballplayer makes more than a schoolteacher for a reason. I was curious to know whether it was a good reason or a bad reason. I don't think my dear Aunt Sally knew. She may not have cared. I think she sort of enjoyed being outraged by the injustice of the discrepancy.

So let's try to figure it out. Why does a pro baseball player make millions and millions while a schoolteacher barely scrapes by? When I sat down to think about it as a child, all I could come up with was that the professional baseball team sells tickets and a school doesn't. The baseball team sells T-shirts and hats, hot dogs and beer, peanuts and Cracker Jack. Most of all they sell broadcast rights to their baseball games. They are a big-money business. There's a lot of cash floating around and somebody's going to benefit from it, so why shouldn't it be the players? I don't know about where you went to school, but the schools I attended weren't what you'd call moneymakers. Intuitively I understood that there was a reason why Tom Seaver made many multiples more than Mr. Seaver, my junior high school soccer coach (whose sideline was pearls of wisdom). There is a market demand for guys with mitt-popping fastballs that doesn't exist in quite the same way for guys who can run both an eighth-grade science lab and an after-school soccer practice. The cash is on the barrelhead, as it were. That's not to say that teaching isn't important or that we shouldn't figure out a way to compensate teachers for all the good they do. It's simply to say that Aunt Sally's complaint about the unfairness of baseball players' exorbitant salaries was a little like saying it's unfair that birds can fly and I can't. If you were a bird, you could fly too.

As an adult I've developed what I hope is a more sophisticated understanding of the situation. A big-league ballplayer makes more than your friendly neighborhood English teacher because the slugger creates economic value that can be monetized easily and almost instantly. Very few people, relatively speaking, can do what he does. Plenty are willing; few are able. His productivity—in an economic sense, not a baseball one—is what determines his pay. A teacher creates economic value, no doubt about that, but it materializes only in the very long term (maybe not at all) and is almost impossible to trace back to its source. And those who stand to benefit most from that value creation—namely, the students themselves—are not the ones paying the teacher's salary, at least not directly. Society pays up front for a hard-to-quantify benefit that only materializes, if it does materialize, over a long time horizon. Not a recipe for a high labor price.

Also, there is a robust supply of people willing and able to do the teacher's job, a fact that can't help but depress his wages. An individual teacher's qualifications are not all that unique, to be honest, and his contributions to a difficult-to-define measure of success are fuzzy at best. Finally, the people paying the ballplayer and the people paying the teacher operate under extremely different market dynamics. A professional baseball team is a privately owned profit-seeking enterprise, often with a local monopoly on its fan base. There appears to be almost no limit to the amount of money fans will throw at a team for tickets, hats, beer, and hot dogs. All this, plus the revenue from broadcast rights, can be made available for player contracts. A school district, by contrast, is a public entity, mostly reliant on local property tax revenue to operate, and thus subject to political pressures from its community to keep costs down. Sure, there's some competition for talent, and rich towns can pay their teachers more than poor towns can, but there's no way any town in America could afford to pay a teacher what a ballplayer makes without bankrupting the school budget.

Aunt Sally wasn't too interested in all of this. She was concerned with the bottom line: The New York City teacher with the most education and experience earned a maximum of $128,657 in 2021; a Major League rookie with no track record to speak of earned $570,500. Aunt Sally would have liked to disrupt these market dynamics, to bend them toward a conception of justice shared by many who hate markets and their occasional vexatious outcomes. All she wanted was for teachers to be paid more and ballplayers to be paid less. She never stopped to think about how this could be achieved or what effect it would have in practice. But I did.

Play the Game

Let's say there was a law—a price ceiling on pay for professional athletes, and not a high one but a dramatically low limit on allowable salaries. For the sake of argument, let's also say that the same government that passed this law was also remarkably smart about shoring up possible workarounds so that leagues and teams couldn't offer non-salary compensation (like boats or vacations or stock) rich enough to make up for the showstopping but now-illegal pay packages. Major League Baseball and the rest of the leagues would collapse, as their best players—the ones who fill the seats with paying customers—would seek their fortunes elsewhere. No one wants to pay $150 for a ticket to watch amateurs compete, and no one will buy an expensive subscription to a cable channel devoted to what amounts to a high school team. "Wages and salaries serve the same economic purposes as other prices—that is, they guide the utilization of scarce resources which have alternative uses," wrote Thomas Sowell in *Basic Economics*. Professional athletes are no different than other workers. They respond to incentives. They go where their talents are valued. They invest in developing their skills in the expectation of a reward. If the possibility of a handsome salary is taken off the table, they will do what any worker would do and pursue other opportunities.

So now that this imaginary government has obliterated the concept of professional sports by outlawing high salaries, how will it go about paying teachers the high salaries people like my dear Aunt Sally say they deserve? Let's assume that the government uses tax revenue to pay teacher salaries. The taxable wealth destroyed by government decree could perhaps migrate elsewhere. All those talented hitters and pitchers could rededicate their lives to other productive uses for which they are legally allowed to make big bucks. If that happens the government could find itself unaffected by the revenue loss from the destruction of the sports leagues, in which case it could simply decide to finance the new high teacher salaries by taking the money away from some other current government expenditure. A hard choice, but one they could make. But the government doesn't need simply to replace the revenue it lost when it outlawed high baseball salaries. It needs to bring in more tax revenue than it did before. To destroy the wealth it once taxed to pay for teacher salaries and simultaneously raise those salaries, the government would need formerly rich athletes to find new jobs that pay more than what they earned as baseball players. Only then could those ex-ballplayers contribute more in taxes after their league was decimated than they did before.

What are the chances of that happening? What are the chances that the net result of this government intervention in the labor market will produce an outcome that makes my dear Aunt Sally happy? After all, we are talking about coercing people into doing jobs for which they may not be perfectly suited. We are talking about depriving consumers of utility that they clearly derive from watching overpaid athletes in tight pants and baseball caps. We are crossing our fingers in forlorn hope that outlawing a certain market transaction will somehow increase the overall wealth of society, which can then be taxed and redistributed to purposes more noble than mere sporting diversions. What are the chances?

I'll tell you what they are. The chances of that happening are about as good as the chances of yours truly playing center field for the Yankees on Opening Day next year. I've always wanted to know what it feels like to wear the pinstripes, but life is not determined by what you want. Some people choose to devote their lives to playing baseball in hopes of making the big leagues. Others choose to play with words and ideas all day. Still others choose to become teachers. Life is determined by the choices we make.

CHAPTER 8

BUSINESS

In a market economy, production and prices are determined by competition among privately owned businesses. These private businesses, as economist Tyler Cowen has noted, make the things we enjoy and consume. They cure diseases and make it possible to fly from Miami to Seattle in an afternoon. They offer services from laundry to hair styling to auto repair to entertainment at every price point. They provide funding to the government in the form of taxes. They also give most of us jobs. You'd think that doing all these things would make business and industry popular. Why, then, are they always such a punching bag?

I suppose the easy answer is that individual businesses often get caught doing stupid and unhelpful things, like stealing, polluting the environment, conspiring to limit competition, aggressively lobbying politicians for favorable treatment, and, frequently, speaking out against the very market principles that serve to benefit both them and society. All this stuff is ugly and unfortunate, even if it is occasionally legal. This bad behavior puts many people off private business as a societal institution. The knuckleheaded tendencies of many businessmen even put off notable free market apologists, from Milton Friedman to Thomas Sowell. "Knowing how to run a business is not the same as understanding the larger and very different issues involved in understanding how the economy as a whole affects the population as a whole," wrote Sowell, who claimed to have offered an A to any student in his economics classes who could find an example of Adam Smith speaking favorably of businessmen in *The Wealth of Nations*. "None ever did."

Smith himself feared that the joint-stock company would become a magnet for dishonest and negligent managers content to run their businesses into the ground so long as they could successfully feather their own nests. I guess you could say that it has happened a time or two. In so much as corporations are run by people, we probably have to accept that a certain amount of malfeasance will always exist in a market system, just as a certain amount of greed and a certain amount of charity and a certain amount of envy will always exist.

Businesses reflect all the complexity that you'd expect to find in any human endeavor. All the good, all the bad, and all the in-between. But we also probably have to acknowledge that in the 250 years since Smith wrote *The Wealth of Nations*, legal and regulatory standards combined with corporate transparency have evolved to constrain some of the more egregious business excesses. New industries and new actors will always pop up. There will always be someone looking to gain an edge by bending or ignoring the rules, but that's not to say that business is irredeemable or that markets are a moral vacuum. Rather, look at it the way James Madison did: If men were angels, no government would be necessary.

Let's stipulate that business and markets are not the same thing, just as interstate highways and the vehicles that use them aren't the same thing. Highways, like markets, are indispensable to the life of the nation. Workers use highways to commute to their jobs, families use them to get from here to there, tourists use them to see the country, and companies use them to ship goods over long distances. Without highways, everything from going to see grandma to ordering clothes through Amazon would take longer and cost more.

Highways are integral to modern life. We would be a different country without them. But people also drive too fast on highways. Reckless and selfish people weave in and out of traffic. Long-haul truckers fall asleep at the wheel, putting themselves and others in danger. Highways are sometimes the location of 35-car pileups that kill innocent people. What are we going to do, get rid of highways? I'm sure some anti-car people thrill to the idea but we can't. We need highways. They are the best way we've come up with so far for getting from the mountain to the prairie and from sea to shining sea without leaving the ground. As drivers, we take note of the risk and do our best to follow the rules of the road. So it is with markets and the businesses that operate within them, or so it should be.

On the Social Benefits of Business

In my high school there was a student club called the Future Business Leaders of America. I was always fascinated by its existence. While I was off rehearsing with the drama club or taking batting practice with the baseball team, some of my fellow students were doing... what exactly? I had no idea. The best my imagination could come up with was a room full of Alex P. Keatons drawing up résumés and business plans and sharing leads on summer jobs. Who knows? Maybe they were reading the *Wall Street Journal* out loud to each other. Whatever it was, I thought the whole idea a joke. The home I was raised in wasn't what you'd call "business friendly."

My parents were great people. I loved them dearly, and I miss them every day. They were thoroughgoing 20th-century American liberals in the mode of FDR and JFK—patriotic, hardworking, fair-minded, and driven by a sincere concern for the types of issues that we have since come to label social justice. They objected vehemently to being lumped in with Communists. They weren't "pinkos," as my dad might say, although as the years went by they became less bothered by having their views classified as socialist. My parents were midcentury American Democrats, pure and simple. Old-fashioned liberals. They believed in the promise of America but felt that it hadn't fully been delivered on for a lot of people, which, to be fair, it hadn't then and hasn't today. Bridging the gap between the promise and the reality, in their view, was the government's job—and its purpose.

It won't surprise you to learn that my parents were *New York Times* readers. They took it on faith that whatever was printed in the *Times*'s pages was the truth and nothing but the truth. So if the *Times* called Ronald Reagan "a lazy and inattentive man, sometimes dreamily disengaged from reality"—as it did in an editorial on New Year's Day 1989—my parents simply nodded their heads, sipped their coffees, and basked in their satisfying agreement. They were disinclined to share the view of Robert L. Bartley, the editorial page editor of the *Wall Street Journal* during the 1980s, who described the Reagan-era economy as "seven fat years." The rising tide of prosperity had lifted my parents' boat considerably by then, but they were constitutionally incapable of giving the president and his policies any credit. "American economic history is a story of booms fading into resentment," wrote Bartley.

My parents erected in their minds, I believe, a wall of separation between economic affairs and the things they felt truly mattered: home, family, helping people. The dirty business of making a living was, in their minds, a thing apart from real life, a separate realm. They were book lovers, keen on politics, but disinclined to think that the business of America was business, that the best antipoverty program is a job, or that a rising tide lifts all boats. Peace through strength, low taxes, and limited government—what you might broadly call the Reagan program—simply horrified them. They didn't think they were raising any future business leaders of America, that's for sure.

Newsweek and *Time* were also banging around our house, and I imbibed from the writers I read in those magazines (and the *Times*) a fair amount of what might fairly be called demand-side economics: high taxes, high regulation, strong unions, high wages, robust entitlements, and a healthy dollop of central planning. Corporations, if left to their own devices, would cheat, pollute, poison, and monopolize. Ordinary people were no match for their power. The clear assumption was that the government should be more than just a referee in society; it should intervene in the private economy, sometimes aggressively, usually via taxation and the redistribution of wealth, to make society fairer and more just. It should put people who need a job to work. And it should guarantee that everyone's basic needs are met, from the cradle to the grave. The means for doing this were obvious and could be fully contained in a slogan so simple and omnipotent that it became a kind of prayer for people like my parents: tax the rich.

To be honest, I never encountered an opposing viewpoint during my childhood. Never did any of the adults in my world—including any of the numerous, underpaid teachers who taught me in the local public schools—explicitly express the view that the private economy performed a necessary and noble function and that it was tied in a particular way to our unique American freedoms. The most I got was that the Communists in the Soviet Union were bad guys and that our system was better. I never got the how or the why. And then, almost by chance, my parents became small-business owners and I got an up-close, inside look at the American dream in action. It wasn't quite rags to riches, but it was close enough. It's a story worth telling.

Born to Do Right

My parents were both from the Northeast, but they had met as teachers in Louisiana in the mid-1960s. They'd gone south to try to play a part in the civil rights movement, spending a few years working in newly integrated Catholic schools in still-segregated Jefferson Davis Parish. They got married in 1966, renting a shotgun shack in Jennings, Louisiana, and came back north around 1970. They already had two little girls—my sisters—to look after, so the problems of the big world that they had hoped to help solve took a backseat to the problems of the little platoon that needed food, clothes, and diapers.

They settled back in Morristown, the smallish northern New Jersey town where my father grew up. He took work where he could find it. He did some teaching, he did some after-hours janitoring, he did some bartending, and he did some building. It was respectable work, but always barely enough. My older sisters wore hand-me-downs and, briefly, my parents signed up for food stamps. Things were tight, but they were back where they belonged, with my father's extended family nearby to help fill the gaps.

Around the time I was born in 1973, my dad got lucky and alighted on a good job with the county government. The panjandrums who ran the bureaucracy were looking for someone to establish and operate a youth shelter for runaways and troubled teenagers, kids who'd had some small-time trouble with the law and for one reason or another couldn't be sent home. One of my dad's childhood friends happened to be a county judge, a well-respected man. He nominated my dad for the position.

My dad had a reputation as a good guy and a hard worker. He'd been a high school football star and was voted class clown by his peers. He had gone to college locally and was everybody's pal. This made him the right person for a government job that someone, somewhere, thought of as a plum. To do it right, however, would require long hours at low pay and—the worst part—being constantly on call for midnight breakouts when the erstwhile juvenile delinquents ran away from the shelter. They gave him a car, a long white sedan with the county seal emblazoned on the side, so he could be available at all hours for emergency calls and meetings.

The job was a good fit. My dad thrived in the position. He liked the responsibility, and he got a good sense of accomplishment from building something worthwhile. It was certainly the kind of job he and my mother considered noble. It wasn't all social work though. There was politics involved. My dad was a Democrat in a county run by Republicans, and he got mixed up in an endless stream of personality conflicts and turf wars. This is what politics often is at the local level. Coaxing emotionally damaged teenagers from the nearby woods and back into the warmth of the shelter in the middle of the night was nothing compared with the constant anxiety that some power-mad little Napoleon was out to punish a rival on the Board of Freeholders by taking my dad's job and giving it to one of his own high school buddies.

My dad was a great one for saying exactly what he thought even when doing so wasn't in his best interest. He was a friend to all, but he hated cruelty and he didn't suffer fools. After nearly a decade of navigating this tricky political world he'd dropped into, he finally rubbed somebody in power the wrong way and, according to his telling, was forced out just a few months shy of qualifying for a pension. It was a dirty business, and as happy-go-lucky as my dad was, he held a quiet grudge for the rest of his life.

Grudge or not, my parents were suddenly in a tight spot. With four children and the oldest creeping up on college age, the wolf was at the door. My dad was almost 50 and he'd lost a good, steady gig. The only income he could rely on was the moonlighting money he'd been picking up bartending once or twice a week at the Washington Bar, a sticky, smoky little joint under the train trestle in our town. He needed a job, and not just any job. Whatever happened next was likely to be his last chance to start over. It was a dramatic moment, of the sort that only happens once or twice in a person's life.

Under New Management

All of that was over my head in 1983 on the day my parents sat me and my siblings down at the kitchen table and told us that they had bought the Washington Bar. For a moment I thought they were going to tell us they were getting divorced or that they had decided to send us away to boarding school. I had no idea what it meant to buy and run a business. It seemed a momentous thing for our family. As I understood us, we were employees, hired hands and hourly workers in those helping professions like teaching, policing, and nursing. We weren't entrepreneurs, not small-business owners, not the boss—never the boss. But now Dad was going to be the boss, his own boss, master of the house. Even if I didn't fully understand what it meant, I liked the sound of it. I think he did too.

The outgoing owner of the Washington Bar was eager to sell and was happy to structure the purchasing deal in such a way that some of the money due could be paid to him over time. This was key. My parents didn't have a pot to piss in. A down payment didn't exist. Most people rely on a bank to finance a small-business start, and my parents got some money from the bank, but they also passed the hat—a very Irish move. Relatives pitched in. So did friends. All of them, including the bank, were betting on my parents to be successful. It was primarily a bet on my dad, who would be the man in the arena running the business day-to-day. Every penny that my parents managed to scrape together was an expression of confidence in their abilities to make the bar work.

What did that mean in practice? What did it mean to make the place work? It would mean, at a minimum, more money coming in every month than going out. It would mean my parents could pay the bar's bills, pay themselves, and have a little left over to invest in the business to make it a better and more profitable venture. It would mean turning to face the wind. No parachute. No safety net. Nobody there to catch them if they fell.

Making a business work means the same thing whether it's Hennessey's Washington Bar, as the new place was christened, or General Electric. The motive is profit—to make a buck. It isn't complicated. Nor is it sinister. Everyone has to make a living. My dad was a well-loved local guy, but his banker wasn't George Bailey from *It's a Wonderful Life*. The friends and family who chipped in may not have expected to make a huge return. Many of my parents' financial backers simply wanted to lend a helping hand to good friends in a moment of need. Some loved the idea of preserving and expanding a neighborhood institution, a place for them to congregate and socialize. They could sit at the bar as Jim Hennessey, the fun-loving Irishman in the Aran sweater, held court. They could boast to the guys sitting next to them that they'd had a hand in the origin of the whole enterprise. But without a fundamental belief that there was a market to be served, that my parents could make a legitimate go of things, then the money they raised was not financial capital but charity, a gift never intended to be repaid.

Charity has its place, but charity wasn't what my parents wanted or needed. They sought to self-sustain. They sought productivity, to take the resources available to them and deploy them in service of building something bigger and better than what they started with. Charity can't do that. Charity fills a hole; it tides you over. Only profit makes what my parents were looking for possible. Only profit can power growth, and profit doesn't exist without risk. If my parents failed, all their social capital would have gone down the drain, along with the financial capital they'd managed to beg, steal, or borrow. There was no halfway. They laid it all on the line.

Here Comes Everybody

I sometimes wonder what it felt like for my dad on that first day, unlocking the front door of Hennessey's and stepping inside as its new owner. It must have been a powerful feeling, frightening perhaps, but exhilarating in the way known only to those who have had the experience of taking their own future by the horns. He'd only ever been an employee. Even at the shelter job, where he got to make most of the important decisions and which didn't end when he clocked out at the end of the day, my dad was always at the mercy of the county politicians. His fate was in their hands. He did a good job for them, but in the end it didn't matter. When they said he was out, he was out. Here, on day one, that burden, that privilege, had shifted. Nobody could screw this up but him. His fate was in his own hands.

In keeping with a long tradition, the first dollar spent by a paying customer wasn't put in the cash register but was framed and hung in a visible location. In fact, there were several such dollars in frames behind the bar, most of them signed by friends and supporters.

"Congratulations Ann and Jim."

"Here's to a bright future at Hennessey's!"

"Cheers! *Slainte!*"

Every time you go visit the dry cleaner or a diner or a hardware store or a bar and you see one of these dollar bills—mounted, framed, prominently displayed—you are seeing a memorial to risk, a down payment on a dream fulfilled. These things don't happen in command economies, in places where some government official decides who does what job and how those jobs are done. The dollar bill in a frame is a celebration of individual initiative, that thing we call entrepreneurship, the explorer's impulse to set off from a known place into the uncharted wild. When you're a kid you think a dollar bill behind glass is wasted money. Think what you could do with a dollar! That was my initial reaction. Eventually, though, the framed dollars behind the bar at Hennessey's looked to me like the American flag that Armstrong and Aldrin left on the moon. They said, "Something happened here because somebody dared to make it so."

The truth is that my parents took the risk of starting their own business not because they had always dreamed of doing such a thing. They did it out of necessity. Given the choice I think my father would have stayed in the job at the shelter until he retired, but he wasn't given the choice. Sometimes you hear people say that being fired was the best thing that ever happened to them. It always sounds great because what comes next is the story of unlikely success. Often left out of such stories is the fear and desperation, the frightening reality of deciding to go all in on yourself, to put all your chips on number one, to close your eyes and spin the wheel as hard as you can. My parents needed to place a big bet on themselves, and the bar provided them the opportunity to do it.

After the initial influx of congratulatory dollar bills, things slowed down considerably at Hennessey's. In the first few months, my parents kept faith with the business model they had inherited from the Washington Bar's owner—catering to the regular customers with a regime of consistency. A radical overhaul could have frightened the clientele. Changing the decor or, heaven forbid, messing around with the range of drinks on offer, could have sunk Hennessey's before it really had a chance to get underway. Eventually, however, my parents began to make the bar their own. Modest improvements to the drinks menu and incremental changes to the look of the place went over well. Most called it Hennessey's, but, compelled by habit or defiance, many continued to call it the Washington Bar until the day it closed forever in 2012.

Everybody Knew My Name

Let me paint you a picture. Depending on the time of day, the amount of cigarette smoke hanging in the air, and the quality of the sunlight that was able to sneak past the neon signs in the large front window—Budweiser, Bud Light, Miller, Miller Lite, Guinness—Hennessey's could have been mistaken for a museum of mid-20th-century American sports. Portraits lined the walls, everyone from Y.A. Tittle to Mark Messier, Willie Mays to Mookie Wilson. Most of the exhibits were devoted to New York–area teams—Yankees, Mets, Giants, Jets, Knicks, Nets. The Brooklyn Dodgers got more wall space than most, reflecting my dad's undying loyalty to his childhood romance with the lovable losers known as Dem Bums. The wall-of-fame lineup was formidable: Jackie Robinson, Roy Campanella, Duke Snider, Pee Wee Reese, Gil Hodges, Don Newcombe, Clem Labine—not barely remembered names from a forgotten era but living, breathing men of action, with piercing eyes and wry smiles, fit and eager, posing on one knee with a pair of crossed baseball bats near home plate at Ebbets Field, rubble now but a temple once, peering out from these haphazard frames over a small cadre of old-timers as they smoked and drank in their high-backed stools and gossiped about what this town used to be. And Notre Dame, of course. It was a Notre Dame bar as much as anything.

It was an Irish bar too. An abnormally large print of a photo of James Joyce loomed near the entrance. You could stop en route to the bathroom to read the 1916 Proclamation of the Irish Republic if you liked, or Robert Emmet's "Let no man write my epitaph" speech, both framed and given places of prominence in the area with the tables where people sat to eat burgers and BLTs off paper plates during lunch on weekdays from 12 to 2. A "Free Joe Doherty" scarf hung beneath the TV. In the 1980s, Doherty, an IRA man, was languishing in American jails while fighting extradition to Northern Ireland. Banners like this weren't taken down, ever, even after Doherty was freed by the Good Friday Agreement in 1998. The frames on the wall were arranged haphazardly. No one put much thought into whether Lou Holtz should be locking eyes with Gerry Adams, or if the '86 Mets deserved pride of place above the Birmingham Six. It was a crazy quilt, an organic visual tribute to the thick bonds of family, community, and common purpose that had created this American bar in this particular town at this point in time.

All of this atmosphere, plus the presence of my dad, eventually made Hennessey's a popular hangout. Initially, the clientele skewed old and male, burly guys with nicotine-stained mustaches, volunteer firemen and cops, paper-mill workers and small-town lawyers, mailmen in their Post Office uniforms, old guys in VFW windbreakers. Some drank Ballantine like it was water. Others used it to wash down no-name rye whiskey or Kentucky bourbon. They all smoked like it was the only thing that mattered to them.

There was no dress code. My dad had one rule: no tank tops, which were a fairly common men's fashion choice in the 1980s. "Nobody wants to drink next to someone's armpits," my dad would say. He wasn't rigid about it. You wouldn't get kicked out for wearing a tank top. More than likely you'd get a free Hennessey's T-shirt out of the deal. "Just cover up your pits."

As a proprietor, my dad was big on a certain kind of madcap ambience. He would "French the place up" with a can of Lysol, running from one side of the bar to the other, canister held over his head, finger firmly on the trigger. This contrail of disinfectant he called the Flying French. It often got a round of applause. Once a year in the early days he'd sponsor a race through town. Runners had to hit several bars in town, beginning and ending with Hennessey's. Spotters were in place to make sure that each contestant consumed a proper drink in each joint. Basically it was a timed pub crawl, with one unique feature: Each runner had to carry a watermelon.

As the '80s wore on things started to shift. A younger crowd began to develop, first on certain weeknights—Thursdays, for instance, which has always been a big night for almost-to-the-weekend drinking. Saturday nights started getting so crowded they had to put a guy on the door to check IDs and throw around a little muscle. As the '90s started to pick up steam, the big night of the week at Hennessey's became every night. It was a place people gathered for celebrations, to lift a glass in exultation after a beer-league softball game, a college graduation, or just a long week at work. They came to be with friends, to chat, to gossip, to laugh, to buy a few rounds, to reconnect with classmates and colleagues, to shoot the breeze with a stranger, to flirt with the bartender. They came to blow off steam, to get whacky, to get right. They came after wakes and funerals to mourn, to toast, to remember. Some came because they had nowhere else to go. Hennessey's became a town square, a communal living room with my dad at the center, holding court, cracking wise, lifting spirits, and doing what he always wanted to do with his life—put a little light into a dark and dreary world.

Some people are standing drinkers; some are sitting drinkers. Most of the regulars at Hennessey's during the boom years were sitters, but there were plenty of nights you couldn't get a seat if you tried. They came from all different walks—lawyers and teachers, contractors and policemen, postal workers and truck drivers. Some owned businesses. Some owned next to nothing. A few were independently wealthy. Some were on fixed incomes. Most were at least flush. The bar itself was a horseshoe, a thrust stage made of thinnish wood but topped by a sturdy orange veneer of some kind of indestructible and easy-to-wipe synthetic surface. The atmosphere was almost always good. My dad hired quality people to work for him—family, friends, family friends. It was a close-knit affair, and customers came to feel like they were a part of something warm and permanent.

To be sure, not everything that happened at Hennessey's was wholesome—some drank too much, they fought, they kissed the wrong people, they fed addictions—but nobody got cheated. Nobody got ripped off. It was an honest place, a clean business. The prices were reasonable and you got what you paid for. If my dad was in a good mood, you got a little bit more than you paid for. Some of the other bars in town raised their prices on St. Patrick's Day. Not Hennessey's. At Hennessey's, regulars got treated with respect. Buyback on the fourth drink. Like clockwork. Anyone who got too loud or too chippy got put back in line, either by the staff or by the other patrons. The community policed itself. My dad helped many people who wanted to quit drinking get where they needed to go. He'd walked that path himself, so he knew how life-changing it could be. He didn't care if it meant he'd lose a customer.

People came to Hennessey's because it was a real place, rooted, a refuge from the pain and confusion of the outside world. It was rest for weary travelers, somewhere to stop, to slow down, to heal. Some nights it would get so crowded and loud and full of smoke that you could barely breathe. Still, the goodness of the place was a by-product. Hennessey's didn't exist to be a surrogate family for the lonely or to provide good counsel to the wayward. It wasn't built to bring joy to the suffering or to fill the holes in people's lonely lives. It may have performed those functions—it did, in fact—but those functions weren't its purpose. They weren't the reason Hennessey's existed. The reason it existed was to turn a profit for its owners, my parents. It existed so that my dad could go to the safe in the morning when he opened the place up, pull out a paper bag filled with wet cash, do some minimal basic accounting, wrap a thick rubber band around the dough and haul it off to the bank. In the bank, the money from the night before would bring his accounts into balance—his employees got paid, his suppliers got paid, his lenders got paid, his insurance company got paid, his landlord got paid, he and my mom got paid.

I Scratch Your Back

Every business, big or small, is the hub of a commercial wheel with spokes connecting to a dozen or more other businesses. Those businesses, in turn, are hubs of their own, with their own spokes, nodes, and vertices. These interconnections are the vascular system—the arteries and veins—of all local economies, which are themselves the building blocks of a national economy. In the case of Hennessey's, there were liquor distributorships and beer vendors, a paper goods supplier and a knife sharpener, the wholesale restaurant supplier, and an outfit that serviced the two giant air-purifying smoke eaters installed on the ceilings. There was the wholesale candy seller from whom my dad bought bar snacks like peanuts, popcorn, and beef jerky. Hennessey's contracted with a special service that came in once a month or so and cleaned the yeasty sludge that built up in the beer lines (a lot of bars skimp on this expense, which is one of the reasons why you should generally stick to bottled beer). Somebody from the jukebox company dropped in every week to clear the dollar bills out of the machine. There was Hans Tailgate, a strange old man in suspenders and German Army field trousers who washed the front window, inside and out, on a semiweekly basis in exchange for $40 and a quick rum and Coke. My dad had a plumber and an electrician on standby, as well as a picture framer for all those Brooklyn Dodger portraits. He bought a lot of kitchen stuff from Restaurant Depot down in Newark. The bakery Hennessey's contracted with would leave a giant brown paper bag filled with hamburger buns and sliced white bread leaning against the entrance every weekday morning at dawn.

After my dad paid his suppliers, partners, accountants, and lawyers—and let's not forget the bank and Uncle Sam—he brought whatever money was left home to my mom, who took it to the grocery store and came back with food for our table. That was the purpose of the business. To pay for itself and to pay for our life. The good stuff—the atmosphere, the jokes, the rest for weary travelers, the furtive love affairs, the friendships, the thick bonds of community—all that was a by-product of the profit motive, which was bound up and inspired by the fundamental imperative driving my parents to provide for their children's future. My parents needed to make a living. The business they built did the trick.

I saw it all with my own eyes—the risk, the reward. I saw the hard work and sacrifice that went into the building of the enterprise. I saw the sweat. I saw the effort. I saw the payoff—the satisfaction and financial benefits that flowed from the investment of blood, sweat, time, and treasure. Our house (the home my parents were able to build), the education they were able to provide to their children, the modest yearly vacations they were able to take—all of it was because of the bar.

I saw the constellation of other businesses that the success of Hennessey's helped support. I saw how they succeeded when Hennessey's did well. I heard the beer salesmen talk about the bonuses they earned from their work on the Hennessey's account. And I saw the social purpose it all served. I saw the fellowship and camaraderie, the friendships and marriages, the loneliness relieved. I saw the hat get passed for those who'd fallen on hard times. There were marriages, golf outings, bus trips to baseball games, watermelon races. I heard the laughter. I saw the smiles. I was there. It happened. I'm telling you what I saw.

Small Is Beautiful

"Stop a moment." I can hear you say it. "All this is fine and lovely but a bar is an easy case. It's a unique type of business. It's not like a supermarket or a gas station. A little bar isn't a big-box store. In those kinds of places you pay for what you get in the hot glare of industrial light, push it in a cart to the parking lot and get going on your way. There is no social purpose at Costco, is there? What great community feeling are we supposed to get at a car dealership, where they rake you over the coals without mercy? Are not the cable company and the electric utility out to screw me over as often and as robotically as possible? Don't even get me started on the banks!"

Sorry for putting words in your mouth, but it's broadly true that Americans think better of small businesses than they do of big ones. Politicians from both parties speak in glowing terms about striving mom-and-pop businesses, valorizing their owners while demonizing the CEOs of behemoth multinational corporations. Everybody respects a rags-to-riches story, even if it's more like semi-rags to semi-riches, à la my parents. Nobody—or almost nobody—respects a giant sucking vampire squid wrapped around the face of the US economy.

Americans are also keen on business stories that feature a single-minded visionary like Steve Jobs dragging the world along toward a new future. We like the underdog quality of a life lived in defiance of expectations, even when we learn that the hero of the story was a bit of a jerk who didn't treat people very well. Why is it that hardly anybody wants to hear about your nice cousin Gary, a lovely guy with a mustache who wears golf shirts and khaki pants? Gary went to a big state university in the Midwest and built up a medical supply company in Texas that he sold last year for $80 million to an even bigger medical supply company. Gary lives now in a large house outside Houston, which your sister-in-law from Los Angeles insists on calling "that damnable McMansion."

For some reason we find Steve Jobs's story inspiring and Gary's story bourgeois and gross, though I don't see why we should. Gary did a smart thing for his family and a good thing for the world by supplying the market with all those medical hoses, pans, pads, and tubes. He could have done something else with his life, but he chose to take a risk and satisfy a real market need. Gary didn't cheat. The world asked Gary for rubber gloves and pill dispensers. He delivered and was handsomely rewarded for it. So what? Why does it bother your sister-in-law so much?

Despite the bad rap that bigger businesses get, there are plenty of good things to say about them. We live in a global consumer culture. Supplying that culture with a steady flow of low-cost goods isn't something that a corner shop or a small sole proprietorship can do. Size brings the benefits of scope and scale. You've heard people refer to the idea of "economies of scale." These are the cost advantages that accrue as production or service ramps up and becomes more efficient. Big businesses have far more opportunities to create efficiencies and reduce their per-unit costs of production, which increases their profits and makes them more able to do the kinds of things that profitable businesses do: hire, create, innovate, invest, and, yes, reward the cousin Garys of the world. You get a hospital in your neighborhood that has the scrub pans and finger cots it needs; Gary gets to be rich.

Hennessey's was a classic small business. It served a local market in a single location, and that location was legally allowed to accommodate about 75 people at a time, though the town's willingness to enforce that limit was often tested, especially on St. Patrick's Day. My parents weren't terribly interested in branching out. My dad had his fair share of offers from people who wanted to be his partner, to help him open new locations. Hennessey's could have become an empire, but it just wasn't in my parents' genes. That doesn't mean that their little business was somehow different or better than the larger businesses in our town. Hennessey's had competitors. Its customers had options. If Hennessey's didn't treat its patrons well, they would have chosen to spend their hard-earned money elsewhere. My parents had a payroll to meet. They had to pay their taxes four times a year. They had to manage human resources, conflicts among the staff. Sometimes they got sued and had to defend themselves. Hennessey's wasn't immune to larger economic forces that were out of their control, like recessions and inflation. In all these things Hennessey's, though small, was not really any different than a car dealership, a bank, or Gary's medical supply company. In fact, Hennessey's wouldn't have been possible without the bigger businesses in its orbit that supplied the discount wholesale goods in large quantities that my parents then marked up and retailed for profit.

You may tell me that there's a humanity and respect in a small business like a bakery or a bar that you don't see in a bigger business. But let's be real. You've been treated shabbily at plenty of independent restaurants and family-owned hardware stores, and you've been treated like royalty by the customer service hotline at Amazon and Home

Depot. And vice versa. There's nothing inherently noble about a small business and nothing inherently ignoble about a big one.

Many patrons thought Hennessey's was special. People get attached to the places where they drink, just like they get attached to the brand of toothpaste they use or the kind of car they drive. We become so familiar with these places and products that we begin to imagine the companies that make them as our friends—or our enemies, as the case may be—just as some did with Hennessey's. People are like this for some reason, and I don't actually have a problem with it. Be a diehard Apple guy or Jeep person for all I care. Or, if you want, hate a particular company or brand so much that you pledge to never buy or consume whatever it is they make. I knew a lot of guys who thought Hennessey's was trash and said they'd never set foot inside. Fine. Just don't fall into the trap of thinking that small businesses are good and decent while big businesses are bad and mean. They are both up to the same thing, which is giving the people what they want while making a buck for their owners, whether that's my mom and dad or millions of Amazon shareholders. In the process, they make the world a slightly better place—just as Adam Smith said they would.

Businesses of all sizes serve a social purpose—banks and big-box stores as well as bakeries and bars. Their very existence indicates a demand for what they offer. When they succeed it's because they've found a way to anticipate what their customers want and deliver it to them at a price that satisfies both of their needs. Just to be clear: I'm talking about legal businesses. Society may for one reason or another decide to rule some forms of commerce out of bounds. I have no issue with that, so long as the decision is taken rationally, preferably democratically, and generally comports with what the man in the street would call common sense.

Many will argue that businesses catering to what are called "vices"—gambling, smoking, pornography, etc.—can serve no social purpose. As with so many questions proceeding from the collision of public commerce and personal morality, the answer is, "It depends." Hennessey's served alcohol, the moderate consumption of which may or may not provide marginal health benefits. The way most people consumed it at Hennessey's was certainly not moderate and probably not healthy. There may be some people in the world who support alcohol prohibition the way others support prohibition of smoking, gambling, or pornography. It's a line for society to draw. A free society will naturally take a more liberal approach to drawing it than an unfree society would. And in a free society there will always be some who say they would gladly live in an unfree society if it meant living in a society free from vice. No matter where the line is drawn, there will be trade-offs. There's always a trade-off.

CHAPTER 9

THE ANTI-MARKETEERS

The world is full of liars. Falsifiers, fabulists, fibbers, fantasists—they're everywhere. These deceivers would have you believe that they are not like you, with your grotesque desires for more of this and more of that, less of this and less of that. They claim that the crass world and its material pursuits don't interest them in the least. They admit no ambition. They concede no calling. They profess disdain for undefined evils such as the "rat race" or "keeping up with the Joneses" or "looking out for number one." The more brazen among them say that when they look out upon the world, all they see is greed, avarice, acquisition, conspicuous consumption, people eating, buying, borrowing, and building things they don't really need. "You can't take it with you when you go," they laugh. Or "I wouldn't want to be like that guy, working all the time, and for what?" Some might go so far as to say that they have everything they need and they want for nothing. But, save for a few religious ascetics, they are not telling the truth. Everybody wants something, even if it's just to be left alone so they can deceive themselves in peace.

The type of economics I've been describing in previous chapters takes as a given that every person has needs, wants, dreams, and heartfelt desires. Top of the list is the imperative to provide for oneself and one's close family. Next, and related, is the drive to improve one's material circumstances. People everywhere are moved, for their own reasons and by their own unique preferences, to pursue happiness by increasing their consumption possibilities. Some of us will even lie and do other bad things to make it happen. Why? Why are we like this? In part it's because we have always lived—and always will—in an environment of scarcity. Some part of it could be hardwired into our DNA. It could be the result of evolution or it could be God's plan. Why we're like this is a mystery; that we are is an observable fact.

A big part of being human is living with the sense that disaster is always just over the horizon. The desire to keep your family safe, secure, fed, and clothed is a noble motivation recognized by almost everyone. Beyond keeping home and hearth together, you may want to get your friends something nice for Christmas or, if you're of a charitable mind, help a stranger pay for college. Good for you. God bless. Whether you are trying to claw your way out of poverty or thinking about maybe buying another boat, a classical view of what is called liberal economics doesn't really care why you want to improve your material situation. It merely accepts that you do.

Classical liberal economics of the Adam Smith and David Ricardo variety actually takes it as a given that we're all a little selfish, just as we're all a little jealous of the things our neighbors have and we don't. It understands that in some deep-programmed part of our lizard brains we always put ourselves first. That's been priced in. We're not all saints, and even saints aren't always so saintly. They struggle with what we all struggle with— our desire to get as much as we can for ourselves, which is driven by the constant sense that there might not be enough to go around.

To reiterate: We live in an environment of scarcity. We can't always get what we want. People respond to incentives. There is no such thing as a free lunch. Life is about trade-offs.

Because it doesn't really care why you do what you do, economics—especially free market economics—has been tagged as an amoral discipline, unconcerned with matters of equity or justice and incapable of processing or accounting for human emotions. Economists are thought to be cold, calculating, overly rational, sort of like Mr. Spock with charts and graphs. It is said that free market economists assign monetary values to things that really should not be thought of in monetary terms, like people's lives. Some go further and suggest that market economics and the capitalist assumptions that flow from it are merely an elaborate rationalization of individual and corporate greed.

These critics have always been plentiful on the political left, but recent years have elevated to prominence a larger number of right-wing market skeptics than anyone previously knew existed. These *nouveau dirigistes* combine socially conservative views with economically statist preferences. Among young conservatives of an intellectual bent it has grown fashionable to argue that profit-obsessed private businesses are craven by nature and that the market has failed to keep the culture safe from corrosive progressive effects. Market actors, they say, must be reined in by a higher power, of which, in the absence of the Second Coming, there is really only one option: big government. Anti-marketeers on both left and right agree that the state should play a greater role in the economy than it does, although of course they disagree on the purpose of these interventions. The far left would like to seize the wealth generated by the free market and use it to achieve progressive social outcomes, while the illiberal right seeks to harness the power of the economy to enhance what some call "the common good." Both feel the market economy is too powerful to be left in private hands.

Clowns to the Left

In September 2019, as he was gearing up for yet another run for the Democratic presidential nomination, Bernie Sanders took to Twitter. "Billionaires should not exist," he announced in that lovable way we've all come to know so well.

The opinion shocked no one. The Vermont senator has for four decades been an avowed and uncompromising public socialist. He has built a successful national political brand around the supposed evils of capitalism and the need to redistribute income from rich to poor through punitive taxation. The simplicity of his message and the regular-guy appeal of his Brooklyn fogy style have conspired to make him a popular figure on the American political scene, built as it is around three-minute television hits and a steady stream of polarized micro-messaging on social media. Bernie Sanders is a character, and America loves a character.

Sanders is one of those politicians that some voters are drawn to not because they necessarily agree with him but because he seems sincere and committed to the cause he's pushing. More, he is capable of articulating crazy ideas in a way that doesn't make him seem like an absolute lunatic. Even as he advocates for revolution he somehow comes across as a decent fellow. In US political terms, Bernie Sanders is the right kind of crazy.

Sanders has benefited from a politics that rewards sincerity, or its appearance, even when the message in question might not sell on the merits. Note, as many have, that Sanders peddles socialism and class warfare despite being personally well-off, even by early-21st-century American standards. He and his wife own three largish homes in Vermont and Washington, DC, and in 2016 and 2017 they reported an annual income of more than $1 million. That's good work if you can get it. That's a revolution most Americans would sign up for.

So what makes a rich man hate market capitalism so much, when market capitalism has not only been very, very good to him and his family but has lifted ordinary poor people by the megamillions out of material poverty? In a word: inequality. That's the issue around which nearly all contemporary left-wing criticism of free markets revolves and for which most of Bernie Sanders's horror is reserved.

Sure, some anthropology undergrads and suburban balaclava radicals still get fired up about uniting the workers of the world and seizing the means of production, but the real serious leftists these days are all about seizing the golden goose and forcing it to lay golden eggs to finance their progressive dreams. At a March 2021 hearing of the Senate Budget Committee, which Sanders chaired, he called it an "obscenity" that "the 50 wealthiest Americans now own more wealth than the bottom half of our society" and claimed that the American people are "disgusted with the corporate greed they are experiencing every single day." He may not speak for all Americans, but he does speak for a lot of them.

Some moderates and conservatives take Bernie Sanders for a clown, a stooge of the international socialist revolution, a cartoonish useful idiot of the global communist conspiracy. I understand why they do. Socialism is a nice-on-paper philosophy that has always and everywhere diminished human flourishing, usually dramatically and often murderously. It literally hasn't worked once. Colorful ribbons have been tied on its head. Lipstick has been smeared across its mouth. Skilled salesmen have taken great pains to try to convince the world that true socialism bears no relationship to communism, or that the numerous bloody experiments in state socialism that stained the 20th century were aberrations rather than exemplars. But the American Democratic socialists aren't entitled to their own facts. The academic differences between socialism and communism are meaningless to the more than 100 million who lost their lives to these warped ideologies in the past 100 years.

If your politics run to the right of, oh, say, Barack Obama, it can be hard to believe that anyone still takes collectivist economics seriously. But they do. Oh, how they do.

Apologists for socialism insist that what they have in mind for the US is not Mao's China, Stalin's Soviet Union, Castro's Cuba, or Chavez's Venezuela. It's not bolshevism or the Khmer Rouge. It's not starvation and reeducation camps. It's not gulags and summary execution. It's none of those places and none of those things. Instead, they say, it's Sweden—rich, fun, efficient, beautiful, polite, and most of all fair. No inequality. Bernie Sanders and his followers want the US to be like the Scandinavian countries, which tax their wealthy and middle-class citizens to the hilt so they can provide "free" health care, maternity leave, and childcare while spending almost nothing on defense.

Denmark, Norway, and Sweden have made the most of an elongated and historically rare period of European peace enabled by the security guarantees of the US military to provide their citizens with cradle-to-grave welfare. Turns out you can do amazing things with an ethnically homogenous society that has been relieved of the burden of providing for its own security (and, in Norway's case, that has lots and lots of oil). American socialists insist that American socialism will be sleek and consumer-friendly. Like IKEA. I wouldn't count on it.

I am not one who regards Bernie Sanders as a clown. I take the old socialist warhorse at his Flatbush-accented word. He claims to be a small-d democrat. He claims to love his country. He claims his calls for "revolution" are meant rhetorically. He says he doesn't want to overthrow the American political and economic system in its totality. Rather, he says, he just wants to spread the wealth. He hates to see people living in poverty when there are so many who have more than they need. Economic disparity is an obscenity. It disgusts him. He would like to confiscate the excess wealth of the oligarchic class he calls "the 1%" and use it to construct a paradise on earth, where poverty would become impossible. He would like to outlaw billionaires.

My problem with Bernie Sanders is not that he's evil; it's that he's wrong. Totally, thoroughly, unendingly, unforgivably wrong. In a world of limits, he thinks he can do the impossible: repeal the laws of economics and redesign the world as he would like it to be, sans poverty, sans wealth, sans inequality.

He can't.

He thinks he can abolish trade-offs and do away with the inconvenient fact that people respond to incentives.

He can't.

He thinks he can short-circuit the price mechanism and the American economy will continue to innovate and grow.

He can't and it won't.

He thinks he can pay for his paradise by confiscating the "excess wealth" of the 1%—and only the 1%.

He can't.

He thinks he can fix up the American capitalist goose so that it will never stop laying golden eggs.

He can't.

He's wrong. He's wrong about all of it. And he'll never be right, no matter how much of a lovable fogy he is, no matter how much of a character he may be.

People respond to incentives, so if you construct a Sanders-style tax regime that penalizes productive investment, society will get less productive investment. With less productive investment, you get less wealth creation and less income for the government to tax. I'm sure you can see where this is headed.

For the sake of argument, let's say there's an optimal level of taxation in any economy that preserves the capitalist incentive—that is, the incentive to use money to invest or build and so earn more money—while also kicking off enough cash to fund reasonable government activities. Early in the third decade of the 21st century, according to Phil Gramm and Mike Solon in the *Wall Street Journal*, America's vast wealth makes it possible for the federal government to provide $45,000 a year in transfer payments to the average household in the bottom fifth of earners. That's a pretty generous bundle to help the poorest Americans get on their feet or, in some cases, back on them. It's easy to be generous with other people's money. Remember, the federal government can't give a dollar to anyone without first taking it away from someone else. So how much more could Uncle Sam give? Bernie Sanders and his ilk think the sky's the limit. From their point of view, levels of taxation in the US are set far too low. They would like to see them raised much higher than they currently are, or ever have been, and think it can be done without any significant effect on investment, job creation, and productive economic activity. It can't.

At the margins, however, Bernie Sanders is right. Look, again, at Sweden. You could raise all sorts of taxes in the US and the marginal dampening effect on economic output and productivity would be minimal, at least at first. It would be the kind of trade-off that the Sandernistas would gladly accept. But at a certain point it'll be one too many pebbles on the table. Every economy has a breaking point. Nobody knows exactly what it is, but if you keep raising taxes on wealth-generating activities eventually you are going to find out.

The Swedes don't seem to have reached their breaking point yet, but indications are they are closer than they think. Sweden may seem a wonderland of progressive virtue from the outside, but the Swedish economy hasn't won any awards for dynamism in recent years. Even before the pandemic, annual gross domestic product growth struggled to reach 2% in a country with more than its share of internationally known companies: Ericsson, H&M, Spotify, and the aforementioned IKEA. An influx of refugees and immigrants in the last decade has put new strains on the Swedish welfare state and generated predictable social friction. Is Sweden's social safety net for Swedes alone? It's a big question with an uncertain answer.

In terms of culture and demographics, the US and Sweden couldn't be more different, but some harsh realities apply to all societies: When an economy stalls out and stops producing wealth and income, it's not the rich who suffer. The Cubans and Venezuelans can tell you what that's like.

Bad news, Bernie: Billionaires exist for a reason. Only a handful inherited their wealth. Most billionaires found a way during their own lifetimes to satisfy a market need so urgent or so consequential that society basically started throwing money at them in gratitude. If Americans are "disgusted" by the "corporate greed" of Amazon, Microsoft, Apple, and Tesla, they sure have a funny way of showing it. Lining up to buy iPads and iPhones invented by billionaires, putting their names on waiting lists for electric cars invented by billionaires, buying $100 annual memberships for free shipping and then filling their carts with everything from fitness trackers to exotic pickled radish jelly as part of an online consumer convenience revolution started by a billionaire—these are not the actions of a people who hate billionaires. For the past decade and a half, the list of the 10 richest Americans has been populated mostly by tech entrepreneurs, people whom the world has rewarded with immense wealth for creating something of similarly immense value that didn't previously exist.

This principle was aptly demonstrated during the COVID-19 pandemic. In March 2020, as the disease was starting to spread and people were beginning to freak out, Bernie Sanders met Joe Biden one-on-one for the final presidential debate of the primary season. True to form, Sanders declared, "This is not the time for profiteering," by which one supposes he meant that anyone seeking to help solve the problem should be entitled to only as much financial benefit as the Vermont senator himself deemed seemly. In the June 2021 issue of *Commentary* magazine, science writer James Meigs offered a corrective: "Profiteering—or, to put it more politely, the hope of earning a healthy return on investment—was an indispensable ingredient in the vaccine triumph." Sanders's tendency to describe the pharmaceutical industry and its executives with words like "corrupt" and "profiteering" betrays a normative bias that could have actually gotten people killed. Life is about trade-offs. Would Bernie Sanders still want to live in a world without billionaires if the trade-off was no Covid vaccines?

The massive push to create effective vaccines minted at least nine new billionaires, as stock in the pharmaceutical companies that developed and manufactured the civilization-saving shots rose through the roof. On the list were the chief executive, chair, and two founding executives of Moderna, a 10-year-old company that was founded for the sole purpose of developing the types of mRNA vaccines that proved so effective at knocking back the novel coronavirus. Moderna had never logged a profit before 2020, operating in the red for a decade before its moment in the sun unexpectedly arrived. The stakes couldn't have been higher and the company, you might say, rose to the occasion. Moderna's vaccine was approved for emergency use in the United States on December 18, 2020, roughly nine months after political authorities started using widespread lockdowns to try to manage the disease's spread.

Bernie Sanders could argue—à la Barack Obama—that Moderna and the other pharmaceutical companies "didn't build that." They got a lot of taxpayer money, he could say, and transported their vaccines to distribution points on roads paid for by the government, so their achievement wasn't really theirs alone. True, but beside the point. Pharmaceutical company executives also breathe oxygen created by plants, but photosynthesis didn't make Covid go away.

The coronavirus vaccines produced at "warp speed" by Pfizer, Moderna, and Johnson & Johnson were the culmination of many long years of private initiative and investment. If Bernie Sanders had his way and billionaires weren't allowed to exist, it's quite possible that Pfizer, Moderna, and Johnson & Johnson wouldn't exist either, and then the government would have no one at which to throw billions so that a vaccine development process meant to take 10 years could be done and dusted in about the time it takes to gestate a human baby.

Pharmaceutical companies take a more enthusiastic beating from the Bernie Sanderses of the world than do most big businesses, probably because what they produce, when it works, can mean the difference between life and death for the person who really needs it. Some view it as sinful to charge money for lifesaving drugs. The people who start pharmaceutical companies are often scientists. Some of them may do what they do because they derive a great deal of personal and professional satisfaction from curing diseases, but most do it because they want to make money. It requires an awful lot of investment capital to find a cure or treatment that works. More money than you can possibly imagine gets poured down the drain before a pharmaceutical company even gets close to the decade-long clinical trial and approval process. Promising research avenues lead to dead ends far more often than they lead to paydirt.

Investors are savvy. They are good at weighing trade-offs. We live in a world that provides almost limitless options for capital that wants to put itself to work. If the pharmaceutical investors and executives who invented the vaccines that brought the pandemic to an end didn't think there was a healthy return to be made in the drug development business, they would have taken their money, talent, and time elsewhere. If the possibility of a payoff were removed, they would have found another risk to take and the world would have been much worse off for it. That's just a fact, whether Bernie Sanders chooses to acknowledge it or not. Although to be fair, he isn't the only one disgusted by the obscenities of free market capitalism.

Jokers to the Right

What is a liberal? In the parochial American political sense the word has for the last 100 years or so meant, broadly speaking, a member of the Democratic Party. When I was a kid "liberal" was used by people like my parents to mean everything that was good about the country—openness, personal freedom, a society that lends a helping hand to the poor, a community that cares. To most late-20th-century Democrats, liberalism meant being smart, educated, and curious about the world beyond America's shores, and standing against an attitude of intolerance and the stifling bourgeois conformity of the suburbs.

Liberals loved being liberals. It gave them a sense that they were on the side of the light.

Conservatives, on the other hand, used the word as an insult. "Liberals" were vegetarians and perverts, or maybe both. They let their kids smoke pot in the house but grew hysterical if they heard the local high school football team said the Lord's Prayer in the locker room. They were blinded by their love of government power, convinced that it could do no wrong, with the notable exception of the Central Intelligence Agency and the US military, whose influence on the world they considered worse than cancer. Liberals were hostile to gun rights, in love with abortion, and made uncomfortable by religious faith that dared show its face in public. They laid blame for all of the world's problems at America's doorstep.

In recent years, "liberal" has been eclipsed by "progressive." The center of the Democratic Party has shifted so far leftward that even Democrats now use "liberal" as an insult—against those who aren't progressive enough. For a student of American history it can be a little confusing. The original progressives were Republicans. The original liberals were Democrats. Now the far left calls what used to be called centrist Democrats liberals, by which they mean to imply that these Democrats might as well be Republicans. The far right has taken to calling moderate

Republicans liberals, by which they mean to imply that these Republicans might as well be Democrats. That's the state of modern liberalism. Classical liberalism offers something else to be confused about.

Classical liberalism, as understood by Adam Smith and the American Founders, is an umbrella term. It describes a political philosophy characterized by an emphasis on liberty, limited government, and individual rights. Classical liberalism elevates the rights of people above the rights of the collective. In doing so it liberates human potential and enables the representative democracy under which we live. In the 19th and 20th centuries the expansion of classical liberalism paved the way for an outpouring of technological innovation and economic dynamism that changed the world, freeing millions from slavery—figurative and literal—and sparking a mind-blowing rise in living standards and life expectancy.

Classical liberalism casts a cold eye on concentrations of power. It prefers the diffusion of power and spontaneous order to which markets lend themselves. It recognizes property rights and grants equality before the law. It asks the government to keep order, safeguard liberty, and enforce laws, but otherwise to get out of people's way. You know when Superman pledges to protect truth, justice, and the American way? Classical liberalism is what he's talking about.

At least since William F. Buckley Jr. announced the birth of modern conservatism with the founding of *National Review* magazine in 1955, classical liberalism has been the beating heart of the economic and political program advanced by the GOP, which is the party of the right in America. There were always rump factions within the Republican Party pushing for this or that deviation from the classically liberal norm—a little less free trade or a little more monetarism, a little less war on drugs or a little more pro-life activism. These were, and remain, prudential matters, open to debate, but everyone on the American right agreed that freedom came first and that economic freedom, in particular, was indispensable.

Now, in the 2020s, there's a conservative rump faction on the rise that won't agree even to that. They regard liberalism with horror, whether it be the classical liberalism of Adam Smith or the triangulating liberalism of Bill Clinton. They reserve a special hatred for the modern economic liberalism of the *Wall Street Journal* editorial board. They are proudly illiberal. While they are driven by their revulsion at the culture's drift toward woke progressivism, the bulk of their ire is focused on conservatives who failed to stop it. They think the Republican Party is impotent on matters ranging from transgenderism to critical race theory. They think America has grown decadent and disconnected because Americans are too free. Of course they think markets are too free and that tax cuts are the only policy that outfits like the *Journal* opinion page can muster the courage to advocate for. They call people like me "market fundamentalists," as if recognizing that economic liberty is essential to human flourishing means you worship mammon rather than God. Whatever. They are very good at calling people names.

It would suit my purposes well if a single figure on the anti-market right could play the paradigmatic role that Bernie Sanders plays on the anti-market left. As of this writing I can think of a half dozen politicians who are angling for the job, egged along by an insular coterie of opinion writers and Twitter polemicists, a handful of no-name professors at small Catholic universities, and a cable talk show host with a national audience second in size and scope only to that of a certain one-term former Republican president. In many ways Donald Trump would be the natural banner carrier for this nascent cabal, but one gets the sense that he has more cabals in his portfolio than he has bandwidth to manage them.

The new illiberal conservatives make many claims against the free market. Like the Sanders left, they believe that unfettered economic freedom is responsible for a host of social ills. The lefties emphasize material inequality; the righties focus on the spiritual side. Some call themselves "common-good" conservatives. They profess commitment to the notion, drawn from Catholic social teaching, that it is a government's obligation to use its coercive power to push those it governs toward the most virtuous version of themselves, to foster strong communities and vouchsafe traditional values. This is not an ethos of limited government. Nor is it an ethos of freedom, for markets or for people. Common-good conservatives are quick to mock those who promote political and economic liberty as avatars of a "dead consensus." Reflexive deference to "individual autonomy," they say, is nothing but "warmed-over Reaganism."

This propensity to deride one of the three unalienable rights in the Declaration of Independence—political liberty—puts common-good conservatives out of step with the culture they propose to rescue. Good luck convincing more than a lecture hall full of Americans that giving up their freedoms is the key to national renewal. "I would die to preserve the law upon a solid foundation; but take away liberty, and the foundation is destroyed," wrote Alexander Hamilton in 1774. The 19th-century abolitionist preacher

Henry Ward Beecher called liberty "the soul's right to breathe." These are not pornographers or transgender activists. This isn't zombie Reagan talking. Yet to the common-good conservatives, individual liberty is not a foundational American principle or an indispensable element of our national identity but merely an accelerant of the social decay they abhor.

Concerns abound in their essays and tweets for the moral poverty that capitalism in particular is said to engender. Economic freedom, with its emphasis on choice, allegedly draws people away from their own best interests (as nebulously defined by the common-good conservatives). The policy program, if you can call it that, is short on specifics. The most you can say is that it revolves around state action to ensure the common good. On social policy they are traditionalist: pro-life, pro-family, anti-woke. On economics they are *dirigiste*—that is, they promote government intervention in the private market to support outcomes that they call "worker friendly": pro-planning, pro-redistribution, anti-business. They want an industrial policy, so they can pick winners and protect certain industries from competition. They want power.

In theory these policies are intended to shore up damaged communities and reinforce traditional social structures. In practice they are indistinguishable from the Bernie Sanders program of high minimum wages, powerful labor unions, trade protectionism, low immigration, and a tax policy that is tilted toward achieving social ends. Call the common-good conservatives pro-life socialists. They won't mind.

Professional economists are usually either classical liberals or French. The common-gooders are neither, which is fine, but why are they so aggressive? Why so confident that they have all the answers? They laud work and lionize workers but speak ill of markets and anathematize employers, as if good jobs can be grown in test tubes and businesses will hire people to do work that isn't productive simply to satisfy some hazy notion of the common good. Some call themselves nationalists, or national conservatives, but don't seem terribly in touch with the nation. They pick fights with regular conservatives, their natural allies, and then pat themselves on the backs for being confrontational. They bash the so-called "dead consensus" for its policy mistakes but ignore the possibility that meddling in the market will produce unintended consequences. They lack humility. Like the Sanders left, they recognize no limit to what government can do or design.

"As we ought to have learned from the Great Society, well-intentioned government policies can do immense damage to families and communities," writes my colleague Bill McGurn in a 2020 *Wall Street Journal* column. "Unfortunately, when it comes to getting the toothpaste back in the tube, government has shown much less success."

The common-gooders' assumption is shared by all who seek to repeal the laws of economics: *This time will be different.* They believe their interventions will be so benevolent and effective that no one will miss the free market when it's gone.

One great feature of life in a society built around liberty is the ability of people with competing ideas about what constitutes the common good to hash out their differences in public through the exercise of their civil rights. For roughly 250 years in the United States, free speech and free association, backstopped by impartial courts and a tradition of basic fairness, have amply demonstrated their worth. They were designed to protect individual rights against encroachment by the power of the state. Pushing the institutions of government to define the collective common good and then promote it is a project practically begging to be hijacked by those who don't share your definition of the common good. Once the state is empowered to meddle in people's lives, the toothpaste is out of the tube. The next guy who comes along will use it to brush his teeth. The road to tyranny is littered with empty toothpaste tubes.

The opportunity to do great things and reap the rewards is another blessing of liberty. The hope of success and a clear path to achieve it liberates the entrepreneurial spirit. It affords creative, competitive, and naturally ambitious people productive outlets for their energies. A society that grants government radical powers to constrain economic freedom offers no roadmap for strivers, no pathway for the upwardly mobile, no freedom to pursue an idea or chase an aspiration as far as you can take it. In a society that bans certain forms of expression or commerce on grounds that they are injurious to the common good, however it's defined, you get not the contentment and stability that the common-gooders imagine but rather frustration, defeatism, sloth, and resentment. You get the sour aroma of dreams deferred.

This does not mean anything goes. Of course a liberal society has the right to craft community standards or pass and enforce laws governing personal behavior. Liberalism does not lead inevitably to anarchy. But the general principle guiding American justice is that the people have the right to do what they want so long as they don't infringe on the rights of others. For the concept of individual rights to mean anything, the government's power over people's decisions about who to be, how to be, and what to do with their lives must be limited. Yes, it will produce outcomes you don't like. Sorry. That's the price of freedom.

"There's a clear cause and effect here that is as neat and predictable as a law of physics: As government expands, liberty contracts," said President Reagan. That's why the plain-vanilla conservatives so loathed by the common-gooders have always opposed the growth of government. Not because government can't do good things. It can. But because the notion that some petty bureaucrat knows your own interests better than you do is both empirically false and philosophically unacceptable. It doesn't matter if the petty bureaucrat is a woke true believer or a common-good conservative. If there's one thing Americans of all political stripes agree on it's that they want, as much as possible, to be left alone.

The common-gooders also play down the moral good brought about by the free market. Markets encourage industry and thrift. They discourage idleness, which contributes to so many of the social pathologies that trouble the minds of the illiberal right's most prominent intellectuals. Much of the time, markets punish dishonesty and corruption. Government intervention, on the other hand, encourages envy, lethargy, and a general attitude of "I got mine."

Rising Tides

Everyone unhappy with the private market is unhappy in their own way. The Bernie Sanders left is disgusted by the concentrations of wealth the market enables. The common-good conservatives are horrified by the moral perversions the market tolerates. My parents were suspicious of the market because it seemed disconnected from the spirit of selflessness that they thought should guide people's life choices. My dear Aunt Sally hated to see ballplayers making many multiples of a teacher's salary. The charge leveled at the market most frequently is that it encourages and rewards greed. As the late *Wall Street Journal* editorial page editor Robert Bartley noted, however, what people call greed is merely an excess of a normal human impulse to provide for oneself and one's family. The great trick of the market is that it manages to harness that impulse and use it to generate wealth that benefits everyone, not just the individual worker, investor, or entrepreneur.

I called it a trick, but it might just as easily be called a miracle. All of society benefits from the virtuous cycle that the miracle of the market makes possible.

"The problem for capitalism and capitalists is that the better the system works, the more evidence there is to suggest excess," Bartley explained in *The Seven Fat Years*, his economic history of the Reagan era. "Depressions do not bring accusations of greed; booms do."

When markets work their magic, the wealth that is created often isn't distributed evenly. Those at the top of the income distribution usually do better than those at the bottom. The preferred cure for the greed of private market actors is to use the taxing power of the government to confiscate wealth and spread it around through publicly funded social programs. It's a fine theory, though boggled in practice by corruption, inefficiency, and bureaucratic ineptitude. Before the government can spend a dollar, it must first remove that dollar from the private economy or borrow it from the taxpayers of the future. No matter how it is obtained, some portion of that government-spent dollar evaporates in the form of transaction costs and allocative inefficiency. This "deadweight loss" makes society worse off in an absolute sense but leaves the redistributors feeling really very good about themselves. They have struck a blow for fairness.

Ed Lazear, the noted labor economist and Stanford professor, was chairman of the Council of Economic Advisers during George W. Bush's second term and a frequent contributor to the *Wall Street Journal*. But I never met him. We never even spoke on the phone. We had the kind of relationship that writers have with their editors—we exchanged pleasantries via email along with small textual changes and suggestions for improvements.

One of the quirks of working for the editorial page of a daily newspaper is that you acquire a large collection of digital correspondents, many of whom feel like friends though you've never met in person. Given the page's prominence, a fair number of our contributors are eminent people and newsmakers like Ed Lazear. Sometimes they get appointed or elected to big political jobs, and you feel a strange pride—strange because you don't actually know them. Sometimes they get wrapped up in public controversies, and again, strangely, you feel compelled to defend your digital long-distance friend. Then, sometimes, they die, which is the strangest feeling of all.

Ed Lazear died just before Thanksgiving 2020. He was 72 and had pancreatic cancer. The Review & Outlook column, which is the *WSJ*'s unsigned editorial voice, eulogized him: "Free markets and the laws of economics need frequent defense and explanation, and that cause is worse off after the death this week of Edward P. Lazear." I didn't write those words, but I do endorse them. I also find them moving, in part because they are true but also because at the time they appeared in the paper I had already begun working on this book, the purpose of which is to do just that—defend and explain free markets and the laws of economics.

Ed Lazear's life story was itself a defense of free markets and the human improvements and accomplishments they make possible. His father was a janitor. His mother sold jewelry at a chain store. In the course of a single generation, Ed went from working in the mailroom of a hospital to working in the White House—a trajectory that we rightly celebrate not because it can only happen in America but because it so *frequently* happens in America. Market capitalism isn't perfect—what economic arrangement is?—but I defy you to name an alternative that allows people to follow the course they set for themselves as far as talent and ambition will carry them, regardless of race, color, creed, or family name. The circumstances of your birth don't matter in an environment that rewards effort and encourages personal improvement. In the long scope of human history, the upward mobility enabled by free markets is rare—so rare you could only call its existence here and now a miracle. We're all luckier than any of us realize to be living inside a miracle.

CHAPTER 10

GRAVITATION

Murray Rothbard was an American economist of the Austrian school and a prominent midcentury libertarian. A sophisticated defender of free markets who described himself as an anarcho-capitalist, Rothbard was in favor of the privatization of everything. He would have been perfectly happy to abolish the state and have private actors and entities assume all its duties from policing to education to street cleaning to national defense. It's a hard thing for most Americans to even imagine, much less support, so I'm not surprised it hasn't caught on outside certain hardcore libertarian circles. Rothbard's tendency to follow the logical implications of his ideas to their natural conclusions unfortunately helped him acquire a reputation as a bit of a kook. The bow ties and rumpled suits he wore didn't help.

Rothbard was prolific—enviably so. He wrote dozens of books and hundreds of essays and articles, and he gave speeches and lectures that have been collected and quoted at length. One of his lasting legacies is the following statement: "It is no crime to be ignorant of economics, which is, after all, a specialized discipline and one that most people consider to be a 'dismal science.' But it is totally irresponsible to have a loud and vociferous opinion on economic subjects while remaining in this state of ignorance."

I don't think Murray Rothbard would have liked me much. While I broadly agree with him on the question of liberty, I'm not the least bit interested in private armies and private police forces. Can you imagine the chaos? Like many libertarian ideas, anarcho-capitalism rests on assumptions about human nature that I just don't share. And I disavow almost every clause of both sentences in that quotation. It *is* something of a crime to be ignorant of economics, as I was for the first 30 years of my life and as many people are content to remain throughout their whole lives. Everyone should be familiar with basic economic concepts. It is my contention that most people are in fact familiar with them, they just don't know it. Economics can be simple. It need not be the esoteric, specialized discipline that economists tend to make it.

All reasonably intelligent people can grasp the law of supply and demand in the same way they can grasp Newton's laws of motion. You need not know, for instance, that net acceleration due to gravity is 9.8 m/s^2 to appreciate the effect gravitation has on your body when you do a cannonball off the high dive at the town pool on the hottest day of the year. Similarly, you need not be able to plot points on an x and y axis graph to understand that the true price of a good is found where supply meets demand. No one talks about the "invisible hand of gravitation" as if it were a giant foam finger pushing people off the ends of diving boards. It's accepted. We integrate it into our understanding of the physical world without wasting a lot of time trying to comprehend or explain it. Gravitation is an invisible force but its effects are visible, just like the price mechanism.

Here's the thing to remember about gravitation: You can't fight it. Its effects can be quantified and observed but they can't be changed. You can try to defy gravity as you step off the high dive but, unless you have the ability to travel at the speed of light or make yourself small enough to enter the quantum realm, you won't have much success overcoming the force that pulls you down at 9.8 m/s^2. It's the same with the price mechanism. If you try to fight it, you will lose.

The more I think about it, the angrier I get at the nerve of Murray Rothbard to advocate for anarcho-capitalism while telling people who don't know what he knows about economics essentially to shut up. One of the best things about being an American is the right it affords you to express loud and vociferous opinions on any damn thing you want, whether you know what you're talking about or you don't. Freedom is the right to be wrong. This applies to everyone—even Bernie Sanders.

If credentialed academic economists got everything right all the time, that'd be one thing, but many if not most of their predictions miss the mark. And not by a little bit. Only a fool would lay real money behind an economist's prediction about what the future holds. For one thing, there will always be a dozen other equally well-credentialed economists nearby willing to make the opposite prediction and explain why the first guy got it wrong. These economists can't agree on anything! The grander the claim, the likelier it is to be built on a projection or a model. Whether it's John Maynard Keynes's multipliers or Murray Rothbard's private police forces, most economic models reflect a world that exists only in the pristine lab of the economist's mind.

Mr. Seaver's only credential was common sense. My old junior high school science teacher was a great economist because he understood the simple things. Life is about trade-offs. People respond to incentives. Prices aren't arbitrary. Baseball players make more money than teachers for a reason. You don't need a PhD to grasp that life is not determined by what you want; it's determined by the choices you make.

"It is often sadly remarked that the bad economists present their errors to the public better than the good economists present their truths," wrote Henry Hazlitt, whose 1946 *Economics in One Lesson* is as forthright a presentation of economic truth as you'll find. Hazlitt wasn't a "trained" economist. He didn't even graduate college. But he had what so many economists lack: the ability to communicate ideas with concision and precision. And he had vision. "The bad economist sees only what immediately strikes the eye; the good economist also looks beyond."

Anyone with eyes to see knows the problems of the world are many. Some are the kinds of things for which politicians and policy makers can come up with solutions, presuming those politicians and policy makers understand the issues and are actually interested in solving the problem. There are people in public life who prefer not to solve a problem if its continued existence gives them an opportunity to sow fear or beat up on a rival. Most problems, however, aren't the kinds of things that politicians and policy makers can fix. Where does economics fit in?

As I have previously mentioned, there are some who imagine that economics is a kind of imposition on a society, an overlay. Political leaders select which type of economic system they want from an array of off-the-shelf options—free market, command and control, a little bit of both—and try it on like a suit of clothes. If the politicians choose poorly, the suit doesn't fit and the society stumbles on its overlong trouser legs or struggles to feel comfortable in a policy jacket that's too tight across the chest. But if the politicians choose well and the fit is good, the society flourishes. Citizens look and feel their best, moving through life with the confidence of a person who's dressed well and knows it.

This is the wrong view. Economics is not an overlay any more than gravity is an overlay. There are of course different approaches to managing economic problems, but the way to think of economics isn't as a suit of clothes. Economics is no more an imposition on society than is physics or biology. It is part of the fabric of the world. Politics is downstream from culture, and economics is at work in both. A culture that doesn't understand how prices work will produce a political class that thinks it can ignore the laws of economics. When politicians seek to manipulate demand or direct supply, they create distortions—usually for the purpose of helping their own reelection prospects or giving a friend a leg up over a competitor. Some, like Bernie Sanders, say that markets exist solely to benefit the wealthy at the expense of the poor. The game is rigged, they say, and the winner is never in doubt. The only question is how well the winners will do and how much pain the losers will suffer. The solution, then, is for the government to step in and even the score.

By redistributing wealth, the government can supposedly ensure that everyone gets their "fair share" of society's economic pie. As my colleague Holman Jenkins has written, there isn't a metric in the economic literature for "fair shares," but there has been quite a lot of academic work done to quantify the economic effects of deadweight loss—the often invisible cost that accrues to society when markets don't clear. Where supply and demand are out of whack, resources will be misallocated, and you will find a lot of red-faced economists and confused politicians standing around scratching their heads.

History makes a mockery of all utopias. People are naturally inclined to put their own well-being and that of their families above the well-being of others, and if they know that they will be forcibly prevented from enjoying the fruits of their labors they will work less, invest less, and generally start phoning it in. That's true human nature. I'm not here to celebrate or exalt it, merely to acknowledge the fact of it. Anyone who says humans are not self-interested creatures is hawking an idealists' economic vision that ignores observable reality. Such economies are destined to fail, as they always have, because they are in conflict with the truth about who we are and what motivates us.

Have you heard the Jerry Seinfeld joke about the Pop-Tart? It can't go bad because it was never fresh. Individuals have rights that are inherent and inalienable. They cannot be taken away by the government because they don't come from the government. The forces that govern markets can't be abolished because they were never established. They just are. Always were and always will be. You may wish it wasn't so. You may want to live in a world free from the laws of economics, but life is not determined by what you want.

AFTERWORD

Visible Hand was conceived initially as a letter to my children. I thought of it as a kind of Dad's Guide to the Market—everything I want my five kids to know about economics before they grow up and fly the coop. Ultimately I decided that a few too many books have been written recently with that particular conceit holding them together. My children are young and will hopefully outlive me. They are of course welcome to read this book should the mood one day strike them, but they will recognize most of what is contained herein as derivative of the living-room lectures and road-trip perorations they've endured over the years. No one utters the words "Life is about . . ." in our house without someone else finishing the sentence.

"Trade-offs. Yes, we know."

"Writing a book is a horrible, exhausting struggle, like a long bout of some painful illness," wrote George Orwell. "One would never undertake such a thing if one were not driven on by some demon whom one can neither resist nor understand."

This assertion comes with my full endorsement. My previous book, *Zero Hour for Gen X*, was about generational differences in the approach to and understanding of internet technology. Ada Calhoun, who writes books that sell more copies than mine, called it a "tone poem of sorts." I liked that, though I'm not sure what a tone poem is exactly. Anyway, Orwell's dictum applied. The generational idea in *Zero Hour* was something that got into my head and refused to leave until I wrote it down. The same thing happened here. I have ideas about economics that I can't get out of my head. The existence of this book suggests Orwell was right about not being able to resist your demons. I hope he's wrong about not being able to understand them.

As a young man I wanted to be an actor. Then suddenly I didn't want that anymore. I remember the day and the time when the shift occurred. It was a Wednesday morning. Twenty-four hours earlier I'd gotten out of bed determined to have a life in the theater. When the sun came up on September 12, 2001, nothing looked the same. Acting seemed silly, an unserious ambition. Now I wanted to play some useful part in the life of my country. I could have joined the Marines or the NYPD. Instead I went back to school. I knew politics would be my main interest, but what goes with politics? What is the thing

Afterword

that determines so much of what happens—and what can happen—in the political sphere? That thing was the very thing that intimidated and confounded me. I enrolled in Economics 101.

On that first day as a 28-year-old college freshman I was terrified. Economics was everything I had always sought to avoid about school and, to be honest, life. Budgeting, bean counting, saving for the future, running the numbers. None of that stuff was for me, and as far as I knew, that's all economics was. Turns out I was mostly wrong. In my first few weeks sitting in that lecture hall, a universe of common sense and folk wisdom opened up before me.

I hope that *Visible Hand* has in some small way done the same for you. Economics is not something to be afraid of. It's not some greedy, nefarious, invisible hand that secretly rules the world by pushing people around the mall or pressing on the heads of the poor until they cry "Uncle!" It's natural and benign, its concepts are intuitive, and it's entirely within your power to grasp. I hope your interest has been sparked and you'll decide to read more books about economics, some of which I have mentioned here in the hope that you will seek them out. You may now have an incentive to keep up with business and financial news by subscribing to a great daily newspaper like the *Wall Street Journal*. But we live in an environment of scarcity that is constrained by limits, the most immutable of which is time. So get cracking. I don't mean to get all "dad" on you, but every day spent dawdling is a day wasted. After all, life is about . . . well, I guess you already know.

ACKNOWLEDGMENTS

I dedicate this book to my father, James J. Hennessey, who died on April 17, 2020. Like me, he was no economist. All he knew was getting up in the morning, every morning, and going to work, no matter how tired, no matter how sick, no matter how much he hated the job. After 30 years of bouncing around, he stumbled into a second act as a highly successful local small businessman. With no training—and no experience, really—in anything resembling business or management, he built an enterprise that was both profitable and personally fulfilling. He employed dozens of people and paid his taxes. He became a pillar of the community, and he did it all after the age of 50. As a result of his unexpected business success, my father was able to pay to send his three academically gifted children—two daughters and a son—to the University of Notre Dame in South Bend, Indiana, which thrilled his Fighting Irish heart. He was also able to finance the drawn-out prodigal wanderings of his unfocused and academically underachieving other son, who wanted to be an actor but ended up becoming the happiest ink-stained wretch in America.

My happiness mostly derives from having married well. My wife, Ursula, is my conscience, which makes her not only my best friend but my best editor. Her love and our laughter sustain me. Our children—Clara, Magdalena, Patrick, Sally, and Billy—are all the motivation I'll ever need in this life.

Visible Hand is the culmination of many years of reading, writing, thinking, and cracking wise. I would like to thank everyone who had a hand in making me who I am. That includes Mr. Seaver (not his real name) and all my teachers at every level. Most of them probably don't remember having me in their classes, but they should take heart in the knowledge that their labors weren't entirely in vain.

I'm especially grateful to my professors at the Hunter College economics department who first ignited my interest in the subject and who bear no responsibility for any errors either in this book or in my way of thinking. Specifically I'm thinking of Devra Golbe and Partha Deb, in whose lecture halls I had my mind blown again and again. They will surely scratch their heads and say, "Matthew who?" I'd also like to thank Donald S. Zagoria, who had a big influence on my way of looking at the world.

My *Wall Street Journal* colleagues are a daily inspiration. There's no better boss than Paul Gigot, and I feel blessed to be in the trenches every day with James Taranto, Mary

Acknowledgments

O'Grady, Dan Henninger, James Freeman, Kim Strassel, Holman Jenkins, and my main man Bill McGurn. I have learned much from the years working with Kyle Peterson, Adam O'Neal, Mene Ukueberuwa, Jason Willick, Jillian Melchior, Allysia Finley, Joe Sternberg, Peggy Noonan, Tim Lemmer, Nicole Ault, Elliot Kaufman, Kate Bachelder Odell, Megan Keller, Mark Naida, and Brenda Cronin. I'm proud of what we do.

At Encounter Books my gratitude belongs with Roger Kimball, who knows a lot and has impeccable taste, and my appreciation extends to Amanda DeMatto, Mary Spencer, Sam Schneider, Lauren Miklos, Nola Tully, Victoria Acevedo, Rachel Williamson, and Elaina Bals. Not only are they a top-notch book publishing outfit, but they really know how to throw a Christmas party.

Barton Swaim's comments and encouragement were invaluable. Paul Beston urged me to persevere when things looked dim. Barbie Halaby of Monocle Editing offered superb flyspecking.

My dear mother loved books and, though it took a while, that same love planted itself in me. She wouldn't agree with everything I've written here, but I don't think she'd begrudge the effort. I'd give anything to see the look on her face as she read it.

INDEX

Adams, Gerry, 162
Amazon, 147, 173, 189
anarcho-capitalism, 209, 210, 212
anti-marketeers, 177–207; being human, 179; billionaires, 189; capitalism (inequality argument against), 183; capitalism, problem for (Bartley), 204; capitalist incentive, 187; Catholic social teaching, 198; classical liberalism, 195; common-gooders' assumption, 201; conservatives, 194; conspicuous consumption, 178; COVID-19 pandemic, 190–91; cradle-to-grave welfare, 185; "dead consensus," 200; Democrats, 194; economy (breaking point of), 188; economy (state role in), 181; free market (claims against), 197–98; free market (defense of), 207; free market (moral good brought about by), 203; free market economics (critics of), 180; government (taxing power of), 205; government intervention (envy and), 203; incentives (response to), 179–80; "individual autonomy," 198; laissez-faire economics, 9; the left (Bernie Sanders), 181–93; liars (world full of), 177; liberals, 194; market fundamentalists, 197; noble motivation, 179; *nouveau dirigistes*, 180; private market (government intervention in), 199; Republicans, 194; the right (common-good conservatives), 197–203; scarcity (environment of), 178, 179; socialism (apologists for), 184; socialism (success of), 183–84
Apple, 189

barter, 25–27
Bartley, Robert L., 150, 204
Basic Economics (Sowell), 95, 141
Beecher, Henry Ward, 199
Biden, Joe, 190
billionaires, 189
black markets, 31
blind spots, 1
Bryan, William Jennings, 16
Buckley, William F., Jr., 196
business, 145–76; bad behavior of, 146; catering to vices, 175; charity, 157–58; competition, 145; demand-side economics, 151; difference between markets and, 147–48; doing right (born into), 152–55; economies of scale, 172; envy (in market system), 146–47; family-run (example), 155–67; government intervention, 151; interconnections, 167–69; joint-stock company (Smith's fear about), 146; moonlighting, 155; national economy (building blocks of), 167; private businesses, 145; profit motive, 157, 168; Reagan-era economy, 150; small (beauty of), 170–74; social benefits of, 148–52; social purpose of, 175; trade-off, 176

Calhoun, Ada, 218
capitalism: anarcho-, 209, 210, 212; choice and, 15; corrosive effects of, 32; criticism of, 199; description of, 14; exploitativeness of, 16; free market, 15, 17; imperfection of, 207; incentive of, 187; inequality argument against, 183; laissez-faire, 9, 179; as man-made mechanism, 15; modern (father of), 8; problem for (Bartley), 204; supposed evils of, 181
car manufacturer, 121
Carnegie, Andrew, 15
Carville, James, 4
Catholic social teaching, 198
celebrity (economics of), 17, 18
charity, 157–58
choice, 18; capitalism and, 15; career, 131; centrality of, 45–48; constrained, 41; drivers of, 75; economics and, 6, 34, 39, 44, 66, 99; importance of, 77; incentives and, 57, 60–61; information and, 85, 98; lesson about, 38; life as determined by, 37, 41, 84, 127, 143, 213; life direction and, 39; limitation of, 94; preference revealed by, 68; teacher's mural (lesson of), 35–39; tradeoffs and, 32, 94
classical liberalism, 195
Clinton, Bill, 196
command-and-control economy, 92
Commentary, 190
comparative advantage, 123, 125
compensation (fairness of), 135–40
competition, 18; conspiracy to limit, 146; keeping pace with, 20; leg-lift endurance, 35, 36; in market economy, 145; protection of industries from, 199; for talent (teachers), 140; winners and losers in, 29–30
Cousin Brucie, 106
COVID-19 pandemic, 190–91
Cowen, Tyler, 145
Crazy Eddie, 105–6
critical race theory, 197
Cruise, Tom, 43
currency, 27

Debs, Eugene V., 16
debt-fueled consumption, 32
Declaration of Independence, 7, 8–9, 10, 198
demand-side economics, 151
Democritus, 65
DiCaprio, Leonardo, 18
digital currency, 27
diminishing marginal utility (law of), 71, 75
dismal science (economics as), 5, 82, 83, 210
Doherty, Joe, 162

economics: of celebrity, 17, 18; central planning vs., 30; choices and, 34, 39, 44, 66, 99; demand-side, 151; description of, 31; as dismal science, 5, 82, 83, 210; elements of, 35; free market (critics of), 180; free market (shorthand for), 12; heart of, 6; ignorance of, 210; incentives and, 95; key questions in, 6; laissez-faire, 9, 179; laws of, 40, 186, 201, 215, 216; market transactions in, 34; metaphor in, 11; models of, 212; politicians and, 214; state action on, 199; as sweet science, 82–85; teaching of, 18
Economics in One Lesson (Hazlitt), 213
economies of scale, 172
economy: American (Sanders's view of), 186; American (wealth generated in), 117; anti-marketeer view of, 181; barter, 26, 118; basis for organizing, 27; breaking point of, 188; command-and-control, 92; diversified, 134; global, 22, 125; industrial, 120; inflation and, 102, 104; knowledge, 117; Las Vegas nightlife, 55; local, 21; market, 15, 91; national (building blocks of), 167; private, 151; Reagan-era, 150; service, 121; socialist, 15; teaching children about, 13
entrepreneurs, 22
envy: government intervention and, 203; in market system, 146–47; as motivator, 20

Index

Ericsson, 188
Escobar, Pablo, 97, 107

Ferguson, Adam, 15
Fleming, Alexander, 119
Franklin, Aretha, 53
Franklin, Benjamin, 17
Free to Choose (Friedman), 113
freedom, 23, 45; economic, 29, 196, 198, 199, 202; personal, 193; political, 29; price of, 203; right of, 212; sacrifice of, 55
free markets, 214; ambition given by, 24; apologists, 146; capitalism, 15, 17, 193; choices in, 75–76; claims against, 197–98; conditions (private economy operating under), 21; defender of (Lazear), 206–7; defender of (Rothbard), 209; economics (critics of), 180; economics (shorthand for), 12; example (Lego), 92; explainer, 112; fairness of, 30; maximizing in, 72; miracle product made by, 113; moral good brought about by, 203; operation of, 26; political disagreements about, 181; prices in, 98; virtues of, 29; wealth generated in, 22. *See also* markets
Friedman, Milton, 112, 113, 116, 146

Gilded Age, 15
global economy, 22, 125
Godfather, The, 1, 2
Gompers, Samuel, 16
Gooding, Cuba, Jr., 44
government: notoriety, 21; redistribution of wealth by, 215; scenario (work), 141–43; taxing power of, 205
government intervention: envy and, 203; in labor market, 143; in private economy, 151, 199
Gramm, Phil, 187
gravitation, 209–16; anarcho-capitalism, 209, 210, 212; "fair shares," 215; freedom (right of), 212; government redistribution of wealth, 215; incentives (response to), 213; invisible hand of, 211; life (as determined by choices made), 213; misallocated resources, 215; politicians (choices of), 214; supply and demand, law of (grasping of), 211; systems designed to fail, 216; trade-offs, 213; wrong view, 214
Great Depression, 16

Hamilton, Alexander, 198
Hayek, Friedrich, 15
Hazlitt, Henry, 87, 213
Hennessey, Jim, 157
Hesiod, 19, 40, 41
H&M, 188
Holtz, Lou, 162
Home Depot, 174
Homer, 19
How Adam Smith Can Change Your Life (Roberts), 44
human resources, 173

IKEA, 185, 188
incentives, 18; choices and, 60–61; distorted, 108; economics and, 95; importance of, 57–61; nonfinancial, 61; prices and, 95–98; response to, 141, 179–80, 187, 213; in socialist system, 92
industrial economy, 120
Industrial Revolution, 120
inflation: economy and, 102, 104; expectation of, 102; problem of, 98–104, slow-motion, 101, target, 104; in Weimar Germany, 103
invisible hand, 6, 11; of gravitation, 211; miracle of, 23–24; passage on (*The Wealth of Nations*), 12; as way of explaining Smith's theory, 7

Jefferson, Thomas, 7, 9
Jenkins, Holman, 215
Jerry Maguire, 43, 44
Joad, Tom, 16
Jobs, Steve, 171
jobs (selfish-sector), 130
Johnson & Johnson, 191, 192
Joyce, James, 162

227

Kennedy, John F., 149
Keynes, John Maynard, 212
knowledge economy, 117

labor market: description of, 135; distorted incentives in, 108; first step into, 109; government intervention in, 143; price for labor in, 136. *See also* work
laissez-faire capitalism, 9, 179
Lazear, Ed, 206–7
liberal economics, 179
libertarianism, 209, 210

Madison, James, 147
marginal utility, 11, 56
market-clearing price, 87, 97
market-clearing wage, 108
market fundamentalists, 197
markets, 15, 25–41; barter, 25–27; black markets, 31; business need in, 91–92; capitalism (corrosive effects of), 32; choices (teacher's mural), 35–39; competition in, 145; currency, 27; debt-fueled consumption, 32; difference between business and, 147–48; double coincidence, 26; economy (basis for organizing), 27; failure, 30; free markets, 26, 29; household management (economics), 31–35; life (message about), 37; money, forms of, 27; motivator (economic concerns as), 38; scarcity, 39–41; social science, 34; trade, 25; trade-offs (choices about), 32; transaction, 28; voluntary exchange in (inhibition of), 28. *See also* choice
McGurn, Bill, 201
Meigs, James, 190
Microsoft, 189
Moderna, 191, 192
money: as capital, 14; forms of, 27; incentive to use, 187; moonlighting, 155; printing of (during wartime), 103; purchasing power of, 102; taxpayer, 191
monopoly: local (baseball), 140; Standard Oil, 15–16

moonlighting, 155
motivations, 43–61; behavior and, 38; choice (centrality of), 45–48; choice (incentives and), 60–61; economic concerns as, 38; envy as motivator, 20; incentives (importance of), 57–61; Las Vegas nightlife economy, 55; marginal utility, 56; noble, 179; opportunity cost, 46, 54–57, 61; profit as, 157, 168; resources (allocation of), 44; resources (scarcity of), 47; scarcity (environment of), 54; trade-offs, 48–54
Mugabe, Robert, 103

Napoleon, 123
national economy (building blocks of), 167
national resources, 126
National Review, 196
natural resources, 119
Netflix, 39
Newsweek, 150
Newton, Isaac, 9
New York Times, 7, 149

Obama, Barack, 184, 191
opportunity cost, 46, 61; awareness of, 73; comparative advantage and, 123; confrontation by, 94; decision-making and, 61; definition of, 54; exclusive relationship and, 57; motivations and, 54–57; trade-off and, 84; weighing of, 125

Peanuts (Schulz), 94
Pfizer, 191, 192
preferences, 63–77; being human, 66; choice (importance of), 77; choices made (preferences revealed by), 68; diminishing marginal utility (law of), 71, 75; economic decision, 66, 76; economic utility, 65; example (ice cream), 67–71; experimentation, 67; free will, 67; margins, 72–77; negative utility, 75; preference mechanism, 75; prices (considerations reflected

Index

in), 69; scarcity (environment of), 71, 73, 77; utility assigned to, 70; utility man, 64–65
price(s), 79–109; choices (information and), 85, 98; command-and-control economy, 92; considerations reflected in, 69; determination of, 145, 213; distorted incentives, 108; economic purpose of, 141; economics (as sweet science), 82–85; expensive products, 93–94; incentives, 95–98; inflation (problem of), 98–104; just right, 85–92; labor, 101, 108, 136; life (as determined by choices made), 84; market-clearing price, 87, 97; market-clearing wage, 108; market economy (business need in), 91–92; markets and, 88, 92, 93; of marriage, 57; misallocated resources, 96; money, purchasing power of, 102; as musical note, 88; price ceiling (example of), 107; price controls, 96, 105–9; purchasing power, 102; rent control, 107–8; resource allocations, 93–94, 96; setting of, 24; socialist system (incentive in), 92; supply and demand and, 87, 135; tradeoffs (choices and), 94; wartime borrowing, 103; workings of (ignorance of), 215
private market: government intervention in, 199; preferred cure for the greed of, 205; unhappiness with, 204
profit, 12; advantages of making, 158; big business, 172; command-and-control economy and, 92; expectations of, 86; motive, 157, 166, 168; private business and (criticism of), 180; questions, 95; reasons for making, 89; selfish-sector jobs and, 130

Read, Leonard E., 113
Reagan, Ronald, 13, 149, 199, 203, 205
Reagan-era economy, 150
rent control, 107–8

resources: allocation of, 26, 96, 157; available, 84; human, 173; misallocated, 96, 215; national, 126; natural, 119; scarcity of, 38, 47, 82, 92, 128, 141; spending of, 127; wasted, 30
Ricardo, David, 122, 123, 125, 179
Roberts, Russ, 44
Rockefeller, John D., 15, 16
Rolling Stones, 83
Roosevelt, Franklin, 16, 149
Roosevelt, Teddy, 16
Rothbard, Murray, 209, 210, 212
Rotten, Johnny, 79
Rube Goldberg machine, 34

Sanders, Bernie, 181–93, 200, 204, 215
scarcity: environment of, 24, 40, 54, 71, 73, 77, 127, 178, 179, 219; limits (types of) and, 39; markets and, 39–41
Schumpeter, Joseph, 32
Seaver, Tom, 138
Seinfeld, Jerry, 216
selfish-sector jobs, 130
service economy, 121
Seven Fat Years, The (Bartley), 204–5
Sex Pistols, 79, 80
Smith, Adam, 6, 7, 8, 9, 10, 11, 13, 23, 24, 82, 120, 146, 147, 174, 179, 195, 196
socialism, 15; American (claim about), 185; apologists for, 184; communism and, 184; incentive under, 92; peddling of (Sanders), 182; success of, 183–84
social science, 34
Socrates, 65
Solon, Mike, 187
Sowell, Thomas, 95, 141, 146
specialization, 111–28; agriculture (age of), 120; American economy (wealth generated in), 117; barter economy, 118; car manufacturer, 121; choices, 127; comparative advantage, 122–26; example (pencil), 112–17; global economy (drivers of), 125; industrial economy, 120; Industrial Revolution,

229

120; knowledge economy, 117; life (as determined by choices made), 127; national resources, 126; natural resources, 119; new businesses, 122; post-industrial society, 117; resources (spending of), 127; scarcity (environment of), 127; service economy, 117, 121; utility man, 121; worker efficiency improved by, 121
spontaneous order (Hayek), 15
Spotify, 188
supply and demand, 6, 34, 95; law of (grasping of), 211; law of (markets and), 29; market activity and, 117; misallocated resources and, 215; price and, 87, 135; price control and, 96
Swaim, Barton, 14
Swift, Taylor, 55, 56

Tesla, 189
TikTok, 18
Time, 150
trade-offs, 4–6, 18; abolishment of (Sanders), 186; balance of, 6; businesses wrestling with, 48; certainty of, 176; choices and, 32, 94; of countries, 127; heartbreaking, 52; investors savvy about, 192; life and, 50, 52, 54, 72, 82, 100, 128, 180, 190, 213, 217, 220; motivation and, 48–54; necessity of, 38; opportunity cost and, 54; time, 46; weighing of, 24, 49, 50
Trump, Donald, 197
Twitter, 181, 197
tyranny, 29, 202

utility, 92; assigned to preference, 70; depriving consumers of, 143; diminishing marginal (law of), 71, 75; gains (trade-offs and), 91; man, 64–65, 121; marginal, 11, 56; measurement of, 66; negative, 75; personal, 131; rationality and, 72, 76, 83

vices, businesses catering to, 175

wages: depressing of, 139; economic purpose of, 141; high, 151; higher (commanding of), 120; market-clearing, 108; minimum, 200; as price of labor, 101, 108, 135
Wall Street Journal, 14, 50, 122, 159, 196, 201, 204, 206, 219
wartime borrowing, 103
Wealth of Nations, The (Smith), 7, 8, 9, 10, 11–12, 146, 147
work, 129–43; career choice, 131; compensation (fairness of), 135–40; diversified economy, 134; as exchange, 135; government scenario, 141–43; gratitude, 132–34; incentives (response to), 141; labor market (government intervention in), 143; life (as determined by choices made), 143; local monopoly (baseball), 140; pursuit (choice of), 130; selfish-sector jobs, 130; utility (depriving consumers of), 143; valorizing (problem with), 131
worker efficiency, 121

Young, Lloyd Lindsay, 106

Zero Hour for Gen X (Hennessey), 218
Zeus, 19